The Economic Development of Barbados

The Economic Development of Barbados

Michael Howard

University of the West Indies Press

Jamaica • Barbados • Trinidad and Tobago

University of the West Indies Press
1A Aqueduct Flats   Mona
Kingston 7   Jamaica
www.uwipress.com

10 09 08 07 06   5 4 3 2 1

CATALOGUING IN PUBLICATION DATA

Howard, Michael.
  The economic development of Barbados / Michael Howard.
  p. cm.
  Includes bibliographical references.
  ISBN 13: 978-976-640-188-7

  1. Barbados – Economic conditions. 2. Agriculture – Economic aspects – Barbados.
  3. Tourism – Economic aspects – Barbados. 4. Labour supply – Barbados. 5.
  Barbados – Commerce. 6. Barbados – Economic policy. I. Title.

  HC155.7.H73 2006   330.972981

Book design by Roy Barnhill.
Cover design by Robert Harris.

Printed in the United States of America.

*This book is dedicated to Delisle Worrell and Roland Craigwell
for their tireless efforts in the field.*

Contents

Tables

Preface

This study analyses Barbadian economic development between 1946 and 2000. The work is an extensive revision of my previous book, *Dependence and Development in Barbados*. After 1980, Barbadian policy-makers implemented stabilization and structural adjustment programmes influenced by globalization and market liberalization. The book informs a wide readership of the various institutional and structural processes that have shaped the contemporary Barbadian service economy. The presentation should appeal to development economists, students, policy-makers, and scholars from other disciplines interested in Caribbean economic problems.

The book is divided into twelve chapters. The first chapter provides a general introduction, while Chapter 2 discusses specific models by W.A. Lewis and Lloyd Best, which help us to understand the dynamics of the Barbadian economy. The issue of size and economic performance is addressed as well. Chapter 3 interprets the philosophical foundations of development policy and planning, and discusses the economic aspects of the early plans.

Chapters 4 to 9 deal with structural, institutional and policy issues in Barbados. The work analyses resource allocation in the real sectors, and the impact of these changes on the labour market and the external sector. These chapters highlight the theme of the decline in agriculture, and the role of foreign investment in manufacturing and tourism. The importance of finance in the development process is addressed in Chapters 10 and 11. Chapter 12 presents a conclusion and summary of my major findings.

I am very grateful to my teachers at the University of the West Indies who contributed to my development as an economist. I have also benefited considerably from information provided by the Central Bank of Barbados and from my interaction with the Central Bank's economists over the years. I also thank Mia Springer of the Department of Economics, Cave Hill, who typed part of the final manuscript. Finally, I am highly indebted to two referees whose constructive comments significantly enhanced the overall quality of the work.

I gratefully acknowledge the permission of Greenwood Publishing Group, Inc., Westport, Connecticut, to reproduce the following pages from my book *Public Finance in Small Open Economies: The Caribbean Experience* (Praeger Publishers, 1992), pages 152–158, and page 65.

Abbreviations

ACB	Assets of commercial banks
ACP	Africa, Caribbean and Pacific
AGI	Adjusted gross income
ANB	Assets of non-bank financial institutions
BIF	Barbados Investment Fund
BIMAP	Barbados Institute of Management and Productivity
BMLAS	Barbados Mutual Life Assurance Society
BNB	Barbados National Bank
CARICOM	Caribbean Community
CFSC	Caribbean Financial Service Corporation
CIC	Captive insurance company
CSA	Commonwealth Sugar Agreement
CSME	CARICOM Single Market and Economy
EEC	European Economic Community
EGF	Enterprise Growth Fund
FAO	Food and Agricultural Organization
FDI	Foreign direct investment
FSC	Foreign sales corporation
FTAA	Free Trade Area of the Americas
GDCF	Gross domestic capital formation
GDP	Gross domestic product
HDI	Human Development Index
HPI	Human Poverty Index
IADB	Inter-American Development Bank
IBC	International business company
IDC	Industrial Development Corporation
IMF	International Monetary Fund
ISIC	International Standard Industrial Classification
K/L	Capital labour ratio
K/V	Capital value-added ratio
MNC	Multinational corporation
NPQ	Negotiated Price Quota
OAQ	Overall Agreement Quota
OB	Offshore bank
PAYE	Pay As You Earn
R & D	Research and development
SDR	Special Drawing Rights
SEB	Securities Exchange of Barbados

SITC	Standard Industrial Trade Classification
SRL	Society with restricted liability
SWOT	Strengths, weaknesses, opportunities and threats
TD	Total deposits
TFA	Total assets of the financial system
UNCTAD	United Nations Conference on Trade and Development
UNDP	United Nations Development Programme
UNECLAC	United Nations Economic Commission for Latin America and the Caribbean
VAT	Value added tax
V/L	Value added per employee
WTO	World Trade Organization
W/V	Share of wages in value added

1

Introduction

PURPOSE OF THIS BOOK

The purpose of this work is to analyse the economic development of Barbados during the period 1946 to 2000. The book discusses development policies, as well as institutional and structural changes that determined the transition of a very small economy based on sugar at the end of World War II to a service economy by the year 2000. This process was influenced largely by the government's encouragement of foreign capital, especially in the manufacturing, tourism and offshore sectors, as well as the provision of a wide range of public goods and services. The work also analyses the role of financial intermediation and public finance in the development process. In order to understand the sources of economic change, the next section discusses briefly the concepts of economic development and growth.

ECONOMIC DEVELOPMENT AND GROWTH

Economic development is a normative concept. It is defined here as a dynamic process of structural change, which guarantees sustainable economic growth, a more equitable income redistribution and improvements in the quality of life of the population. Structural change was central to the work of economists such as Demas (1965), and Chenery and Syrquin (1975). Structural change relates to the diversification of the productive base, reflecting a movement of factors of production and output between primary, secondary and tertiary economic activities. The degree of structural change depends on the conscious policies of the state and the country's opportunities in international trade.

Economic growth is sustainable if the natural and physical capital stock is not allowed to deteriorate (see Pearce and Warford 1993). Sustainability implies that the needs of future generations should not be compromised by economic progress. Environmentalism and sustainable development have been important topics since the 1980s. However, this book makes no attempt to discuss the wide-ranging environmental issues in sustainable development. The literature on sustainable development and environmental economics is extensive. The reader is referred to Pearce and Warford (1993).

For development to take place, structural change and growth must be accompanied by income redistribution and poverty alleviation. Welfare considerations relating to income redistribution and poverty were assigned a low status in the early efforts of many of the development economists of the 1950s. The need for income redistribution was emphasized in the work of Seers (1979). The disenchantment with the 1950s strategy of growth and "trickle down" redistribution led to a new interpretation of development as a poverty-alleviation process. Thus, economic development should be conceived as an improvement in the level of welfare in a society.

Development policies to improve welfare levels should also emphasize increased local decision making in the economy. Some measure of indigenous development in terms of domestic food production, the mobilization of domestic savings and entrepreneurship should be pursued as a means of increasing the resilience of the developing economy. Further, the pursuit of indigenous development should also be interpreted as the acquisition of a reasonable degree of local ownership and control of key sectors of the economy, such as agriculture, manufacturing, banking and public utilities.

Although indigenous development is highly desirable in small economies, a type of development can be achieved with the use of large external resources. Following Evans (1979), I call this process *dependent development*, an appropriate concept to describe the Barbadian experience. Foreign capital helps to accelerate the development process by financing the deficit in the balance of payments. This point is discussed later when we examine the nature of economic growth.

Ingham (1993) advances the view that the economists' "goods centred" concept of development must be combined with a "people centred" development effort. The Human Development Index (HDI) is one attempt to measure human development by incorporating variables such as life expectancy, the quality and delivery of health care and literacy. According to Ingham these variables show the choices available to the population, the priorities set by the political leaders and the degree to which funds are allocated to meet these needs. However, I believe that a "goods centred" focus of development should be combined with a "people centred" approach.The concepts of welfare and poverty alleviation are indicative of the economists' "people centred" approach to development.

Other attempts to broaden the concept of development incorporate terms such as freedom and political and civil liberties. For example, Sen (1988) stresses the importance of positive freedom to choose. The only problem with this extended approach is that the debate on these concepts is extensive and controversial, and their precise relationship to development may be difficult to test empirically. However, Ingham suggests that countries in which citizens enjoy greater political and civil liberties also perform better in "people centred" measures of development.

Economic growth is defined as the increase in real output and is an important component of economic development. However, growth by itself is not development. Economists have been concerned with identifying the main sources of growth. The vast literature suggests that capital accumulation and technological progress are the main causes of growth. The neoclassical growth theory attributes most growth to exogenously determined technological progress. The newer endogenous growth theory explains technological change as an endogenous outcome of public and private investments in human capital and knowledge-intensive industries (see Todaro 1997:93). The endogenous growth literature also attributes growth to policies arising within the system of production, rather than simply to exogenously determined technological progress assumed by the neoclassical approach (see Tanzi and Zee 1997:180).

One of the main sources of growth is savings, which accelerate the capital formation process. The propensity to save is determined by income levels, cultural patterns and the development of institutions to encourage the savings habit. An increase in thrift may stimulate investment if the savings are effectively mobilized, but too high a level of thrift may retard investment. Governments must also save by increasing the surplus on its current account. Governments therefore need to reduce wasteful expenditures. Dissaving by government often leads to the printing of money to finance public sector activities. Such money creation causes inflation and balance-of-payments deficits. Additionally, if government imposes tax rates that are too high, these may also reduce the level of savings.

The accumulation of physical capital is not the only source of growth. Endogenous growth theorists devote considerable attention to the role of human capital. The development of human resources can lead to an outward shift in the production function. Human resource development depends on education and training, the use of information technology and so forth. Human resource development enables workers to become more productive, thereby raising the level of real output.

Small, open economies also need foreign exchange to achieve reasonable rates of economic growth. Foreign exchange is necessary to supplement domestic savings and to finance imports. Such foreign exchange can be acquired through foreign borrowing or foreign direct investment (FDI). In an effort to accelerate their rates of economic growth, some developing countries import high levels of raw materials and capital goods. This sometimes leads to large balance-of-payments deficits and a depletion of foreign reserves. Severe losses of foreign exchange can cause economic embarrassment for developing countries, forcing them to seek assistance from the International Monetary Fund (IMF). Developing countries should therefore attempt to achieve a growth rate consistent with their ability to earn foreign exchange.

The natural resource base of a country also provides a source of growth. However, it is the efficient use of these resources that determines the expansion of the production function. Some countries with huge petroleum and bauxite resources have low rates of economic growth. On the other hand, a country like Japan with a limited natural resource base has been one of the fastest growing economies since World War II.

Capital formation, savings mobilization and technological progress can only take place efficiently if appropriate legal, economic and political institutions exist to enforce property rights. Neoclassical theory ignored the role of institutions in economic growth. Institutional failure is also a cause of market failure in many developing countries. Lewis (1955:57) asserted that "institutions promote or restrict growth according to the protection they accord to effort, according to the opportunities they provide for specialization and according to the freedom of manoeuvre they permit". Further, democracy helps to build good institutions and accelerate growth. I agree with Rodrik's (2000) observation that local knowledge is important, and participatory political systems are the most effective for processing and aggregating local knowledge required for growth.

To understand the policy decisions influencing the post-war development process in Barbados, some historical perspective is necessary. The next section therefore looks briefly at the socio-economic and political scenario of the period 1937–46. Much of the economic philosophy influencing policy decisions in the early post-war economy emerged in the turbulent socio-economic circumstances of 1937–46. It is also necessary to examine the development policy implications of the alteration in British colonial policy in relation to Barbados during this era.

THE SOCIAL ECONOMY OF 1937–46

The year 1937 was a landmark in Barbadian economic history because it was characterized by social unrest attributable in large measure to domestic poverty and severe depression in the international economy. In 1937, Barbados showed all the conventional symptoms of an underdeveloped economy, with a production structure based almost entirely on sugar, primarily as a result of its historical status as a British colony. The principal institution of production was the plantation system and the Barbadian social structure in 1937 largely reflected the development of the corporate plantation economy (Karch 1979). The society was stratified on the basis of colour and wealth, and the white elite controlled the political system, which gave them distinct privileges in relation to the law. Despite Barbados's dependent colonial status, the planter government exercised some political authority. According to Belle (1974) the planter class in 1937 constituted an independent economic ruling class. There existed in 1937 not a colonial government but a national autocracy that at times challenged colonial authority.

The socio-economic status of rural and urban workers between 1937 and 1946 was one of material deprivation. The living conditions of this labouring class have been well documented in the colonial reports. They can be identified as symptoms of underdevelopment. The incidence of infant mortality was high; low wages and a high cost of living compounded the problems associated with a low standard of sanitary arrangements. The 1945 Moyne Commission blamed these symptoms of underdevelopment on "over-population". This commission attributed much of the high unemployment to technological improvements in the sugar industry and the reduction of emigration outlets.[1] However, the underdevelopment of the Barbadian economy during the period 1937–46 must be seen as a consequence of the historical development of the corporate plantation system, the crisis of the sugar industry in the 1930s and the world economic depression of 1929.[2]

The crisis of the sugar industry in the 1930s worsened the plight of the Barbadian labouring classes. After World War I, imperial preferences and increased technical efficiency enabled the West Indian colonies to expand sugar exports to Britain. However, a rapid decline in sugar prices began in 1925 and was aggravated by the world depression of the late 1920s, which led to high levels of world sugar supplies in relation to demand. The appointment of the Olivier Commission in 1929 brought an increase in imperial preferences and Barbados was able to receive twice the London free market price for sugar, but the price was still too low to prevent the depressed economic conditions of the late 1930s.

The depression in the world economy that began in 1929 led to a decline in colonial exports. Further, as Starkey (1939) notes, the worldwide depression closed emigration outlets and many Barbadians returned home, unable to find jobs. These conditions deepened underdevelopment and contributed to the social unrest of 1937. However, during the wartime period (1939–46), there was some attempt to increase self-sufficiency in response to the food shortages created by the war. Economic conditions remained depressed, however. In 1946, the Barbadian economy remained a mono-crop economy dominated by the plantation system.

Social and economic deprivation of the majority of people was not only externally determined. The legal system reinforced underdevelopment and limited the growth of a freehold peasantry. The system of plantation tenantries (sometimes known as the tenantry system) effectively tied a large tenant labour force to the plantation. The growth of the tenantry system dates from after the emancipation of the slaves in 1838.[3] In order to ensure a continuous labour supply for the estates, the planters permitted the ex-slaves to occupy a small plot of land and a house, for which a money rent was charged, in exchange for their continuous labour on the plantations. In Barbados, the rise of a freehold peasantry was a slow process partly because of the scarcity of land and the legal arrangements that existed under the tenantry system. This system persisted after 1946 but was modified by various legislative enactments.[4] This arrangement is one instance demonstrating how the legal system reinforced underdevelopment, social deprivation and landlessness in the context of the plantation-dominated economy of Barbados before the end of World War II.

The underdevelopment of the Barbadian economy as well as other Caribbean economies during the 1930s was partly diagnosed by W.A. Lewis (1937), a contemporary observer of the economic conditions of that time. Lewis traced the deplorable economic conditions that had caused the social upheaval of 1937, and challenged the vested interests that had depressed the standard of living of the labouring classes through indirect taxation. However, Lewis looked to Britain as the saviour of the Caribbean countries. He argued that it was necessary to increase the price of sugar and that Britain should grant the colonies increased preferential treatment in the form of loans and grants. Even though he stressed the paramount importance of income redistribution and the need to increase total incomes, his hope for the development of the Caribbean was based on industrialization through the promotion of foreign capital investment. This early recommendation, emphasized in his later works, had a significant impact on post-war development thinking, especially after 1960, and differed fundamentally from the views of the 1945 Moyne Commission, discussed below. Lewis, writing in the 1930s, regarded the future development of the colonies as dependent on their power to attract capital. Despite this early line of inquiry, Lewis interpreted the significance of the events of the 1930s as resting in the rise of trade unionism in the Caribbean and the entry of the working class into West Indian politics. His other ideas were submerged in the early 1950s partly as a consequence of the resurgence of the sugar industry immediately after the war, which ushered in a new period of plantation domination.

The economic policy recommendations contained in the Moyne Commission Report had an important influence on decision making in the post-war economy. The Moyne Commission's primary recommendation was based on the old Eurocentric view that the best hope for the colonies was in agricultural production. It is evident that members of the commission confused the symptoms of underdevelopment with its causes. Their exposition failed to emphasize the deleterious impact of centuries of colonization that had led to a lopsided production structure based on the plantation system.

The Moyne Commission felt that although secondary industries could be afforded, they were relatively unimportant. This view was echoed in the first development plan for Barbados (1946–55), which reflected fundamentally colonial development ideals. This plan argued that any substantial increase in national output was dependent on the expansion of the sugar industry.

The central thesis of the Moyne Commission Report was that structural change was not very important in the context of the colonial economy at that time. The Moyne Commission, for instance, did not deem it feasible to recommend that any West Indian colonies should undertake substantial financial liabilities to encourage the tourist trade. It considered that the risks of capital involved in the sector should be borne by private enterprise rather than the taxpayer. Even though British colonial policy changed between 1929 and 1946 from the model of colonies as mere sources of extraction of surplus and suppliers of raw materials to a policy based on the principle of "responsible trusteeship", one can support the view advanced by Brett (1973) that the new "benevolent" policy underlined the tendency of the Colonial Office to promote certain types of economic activity in the colonies, which prevented the emergence of a policy to encourage secondary and tertiary production required for structural change.

My interpretation of British colonial policy during the period 1937–46 corroborates Brett's (1973) view that colonial development was important to Britain because the colonies could contribute to relieving unemployment in Britain. The change in British colonial development thinking which culminated in the Colonial Development and Welfare Acts of 1940 and 1945 had its roots in the depressed conditions facing British industry after World War II. Brett (1973:116) writes:

> The colonies could be made to contribute directly to British industry – to keeping the workforce employed, and the profits high; equally important, by doing this the colonies could also contribute to political stability.

Indeed, the colonial welfare legislation of the 1940s, which was a consequence of the West Indian disturbances of 1937–38, recognized that the colonies would become better markets for British products. Colonial economic revival was therefore linked with metropolitan prosperity. The Welfare Acts were also designed to stimulate the growth of the social services based on the view of the Colonial Office that a colony should have only those services that it could finance from its own immediate resources (see Johnson 1977).

Finally, if the change in British development philosophy was not designed to promote meaningful structural change in the colonies, the persistence after 1937 of a planter–merchant alliance in Barbados reinforced a type of economic dependence based on sugar monoculture.[5] This alliance, which was shaped by the development of the corporate plantation system in the late nineteenth century, controlled the commanding heights of the economy – sugar and the distribution trade. Even though the planters had lost political power after 1937, their economic control persisted into the 1950s because the pattern of economic thought projected by the Moyne Commission was based on the expansion of primary output. Belle (1974) advanced the thesis of planter–merchant economic dominance. He argued that even after Barbados's political independence from Britain in 1966, the planter–merchant alliance continued to monopolize the best agricultural land and the distributive trade.

METHODOLOGY

Methodologically, this study adopts a historical/institutional/structural approach to economic development. This methodology, employed by many Latin American structuralist economists in the 1960s, is concerned with institutional and structural processes characteristic of the economy during delineated time periods. The historical/institutional/structural methodology is appropriate in the Barbadian context for examining the role of a few important institutions, namely the state, the market, plantation agriculture, foreign capital, the fiscal system and the financial system. Each of these institutions changed over the period, exerting an influence on development and growth. The behaviour of structural variables such as output, land, labour and capital must be analysed in relation to changes in the institutional framework. Further, this approach borrows from institutional economics in recognizing the impact of institutional change on development. See, for example, North (1989). Indeed, it can be argued that the original work of the Caribbean economists of the 1960s was rooted in institutional economics, combined with the structuralist approach of the Latin American school led by Furtado, Sunkel and others.

This study divides the post–World War II period into the period of colonial development (1946–60), the service economy period (1960–91), and the period of crisis and structural adjustment (1991–2000). The service economy persisted after 1990, but the third period was characterized by a new emphasis on market-oriented development, influenced by neoliberalism and globalization. For ease of exposition I often refer to the actual time periods or specific years, rather than the names designated to the periods. Let us look at the salient features of these three periods.

The period of colonial development saw the transition to representative government and political independence. It was characterized by a new emphasis by the British government on welfare and planning in the colonies, a phase sometimes described by the metropolitan power as "responsible trusteeship". In keeping with the prevailing philosophy of "neo-mercantilism", the colonial state adhered to a policy of monoculture sanctioned by the "official classes" of colonial society, such as the planter–merchant class and the colonial bureaucracy. The resurgence of the sugar industry was due partly to the conscious policy of the state, labour-displacing technological advance, as well as the strengthening of the alliance between the plantocracy and mercantile interests.

In the service economy period, with the completion of gradualist decolonization, the state became allied to foreign capital. That is, the Barbadian government adopted W.A. Lewis's (1950) Puerto Rican model (discussed in Chapter 2), sometimes known as "industrialization by invitation", and promoted a wide range of tourism and financial services made possible by the inflow of foreign capital. Lewis's operational model was possible largely as a result of the economic infrastructure provided during the period of colonial development. However, the Lewis model was a distinct break from the colonial model that advocated agricultural specialization. In this period, also, successive governments placed more emphasis on the welfare needs of the Barbadian people. This era also saw policy initiatives related to state-aided tourism and offshore business. Any discussion of the Barbadian development process after 1960 must emphasize the government's cooperation with foreign capital, as well as the service-oriented nature of public policy.

The third period is that of crisis and structural adjustment (1991–2000). The Barbadian economy went into crisis in 1991, largely due to overspending by the public sector as well as recession in the world economy. An IMF stabilization programme was implemented, as well as a structural adjustment programme aimed at reducing the size of government and achieving market liberalization and tax reform. Globalization and market liberalization explain the trend toward market-oriented development during this period.

Many books have been written on globalization and no attempt is made in this study to examine the wide-ranging issues. Among the numerous contributions to the globalization debate are Klak (1998), Dunning (1997), Girvan (2000), Bernal (2000) and Rodrik (2002). Further, space constraints do not allow us to do full justice to the theoretical issues related to market liberalization (sometimes known as neoliberalism) and structural adjustment. Useful references are Rodrik (1990) and Aricanli and Rodrik (1990). However, later chapters will deal with some empirical aspects of trade liberalization, tax reform, privatization and export promotion in Barbados.

2

Lewis and the Plantation Economy School

INTRODUCTION

This chapter analyses specific models by Caribbean economists that explain Barbadian development, as well as the economic constraints on further growth. The pattern of dependent development in Barbados, especially after 1960, can be explained largely with reference to the conceptual framework and operational Puerto Rican model of W.A. Lewis.[1] A supporting argument is that the plantation economy model, as articulated by Lloyd Best, and small economic size explain some of the constraints on growth in the Barbadian economy.[2] Both Lewis and Best were important in influencing the changes in development policy and planning over the period studied, so that it is necessary to place their work in the correct theoretical perspective.

The Lewis conceptual framework is not simply based on the dual economy thesis. It is anchored as well in the role of institutions in the development process. One of the pillars of his framework is the secular stagnation of the developing economy stemming from the deterioration of the factoral terms of trade. Lewis's model of capital accumulation provided the theoretical rationale for the Puerto Rican model adopted by Barbados.

Best's articulation of the plantation economy model is essential to our historical analysis. The development of the sugar industry in the post–World War II period, along with certain manifestations of the Puerto Rican model, replicated some of the features of the plantation economy model. The chapter will also show how the "rules of the game" of the pure plantation economy were modified in the contemporary period. Finally, we note that the size constraint elaborated by Demas (1965) is not at variance with either the Lewis policy model or the plantation economy articulation.

So far we have said nothing about class analysis. While realizing the importance of class structure change in the development process, no attempt was made to examine empirically class structure change in Barbados. Our empirical work is based on the historical/structural/institutional approach rather than the Marxian theory of historical materialism.

LEWIS'S CONCEPTUAL FRAMEWORK

Lewis's conceptual framework constitutes a consistent body of thought on capitalist development initiated by his seminal article on economic development with unlimited supplies of labour. Additional insights into his theory of the open economy were provided in the Wicksell Lectures of 1971 and the Janeway Lectures of 1978.[3] This section outlines briefly Lewis's main propositions, rather than debates the extensive refinements and criticisms of his original work. In this way we can identify the principal implications for the development process of an economy like that of Barbados.

Lewis employs an interdisciplinary framework to identify the sociocultural factors conducive to economic growth.[4] Although he uses the term "growth", he discusses some broad aspects of development. His three proximate causes of growth are the will to economize, increasing knowledge and capital accumulation. Lewis is concerned with identifying the type of institutions or beliefs or environment that favour these proximate causes. History is utilized to explain why certain institutions restrict or promote growth. The character of social and economic institutions is therefore crucial to Lewis's theory. In this respect he shares similar ground with the New World economists such as Beckford and Best who sought to explain the institutional factors inhibiting Caribbean development.

Capital accumulation promotes growth, but it depends on the emergence of a capitalist class conditioned by the values, beliefs and institutions of the society. Equally significant is the type of income distribution that facilitates capitalist development. The latter cannot be initiated and sustained unless there is an inegalitarian type of income distribution.

Lewis asserts that the main source of savings in any economy is profits, distributed or undistributed. If this is so, then the conversion of an economy from a 5 to 12 percent saver must be explained by an increase in the share of profits in the national income. The emergence of a productive capitalist class is necessary to achieve the 12 percent ratio of savings to national income. The increase in the rate of profit depends on some constancy in the real wage in the early stage of the development process.[5]

This pivotal conceptual point is elaborated in his closed model of unlimited supplies of labour. This model identifies the mechanisms whereby capitalists can increase the share of profits in the national income. The model's mechanism explains the growth of the production of domestic savings in the national income in the early stages of an economy whose growth is due to capitalist forms of production. Capitalists in the modern sector will employ labour drawn from the traditional or subsistence sector up to the point where labour's marginal productivity is equal to the current wage. The reinvestment of the capitalist surplus proceeds up to the level where all surplus labour is absorbed and the process ends. If the capitalist sector trades with the traditional sector comprising peasants producing food, the increase in the demand for food by capitalists will raise the price of food in terms of capitalist products, thereby reducing profits. In this case, it may be necessary to tax agriculture and use the proceeds to finance capital formation.

Lewis also shows that alternative means of financing capital formation, such as credit and government inflationary finance, always move the income distribution in favour of capitalists. Credit-financed capital formation causes an inflationary process that redistributes income in favour of profits. Inflationary government finance also leads the profits of the industrial capitalist class to rise more rapidly than other incomes.

Lewis's closed model is a positive theory of capital accumulation in the modern sector. However, he states explicitly that economic growth requires that productivity in the peasant sector of the economy must increase to provide a growing surplus per head to feed the non-farmers. In the Caribbean context Lewis, like Beckford, has advanced views favourable to peasant development. Even though he argued that plantations were more efficient in sugar production, peasant agriculture leads to greater self-sufficiency in crops other than sugar (Lewis 1936). In our subsequent analysis of Barbadian development we consider the severe constraints on the development of the peasantry as the subsector producing for the domestic market.

The most important point in Lewis's open model is the relationship between real wages in the developing country and its factoral terms of trade. This point is particularly relevant in relation to the behaviour of sugar prices in Third World economies in the post–World War II period. Lewis makes two fundamental points. The increase in productivity of export staples from underdeveloped countries will benefit the workers of advanced countries. Given the deterioration in the terms of trade in the underdeveloped countries, economic development and improved income distribution require an increase in labour productivity in the peasant sector of the economy producing for the home market. The argument is that developing countries cannot escape adverse terms of trade by increasing productivity in export staples, since this reduces the price of such commodities on the world market, leading to a deterioration of real wages in these countries.

Lewis's conceptual framework leads to a number of policy implications that are instructive for analysing development policy in Barbados. The closed model indicates that increases in business profits, as well as higher levels of domestic savings, are keys to growth and development.

Lewis's conceptual framework is supportive of foreign capital in the industrial sector, especially when the indigenous capitalist class is too weak. This was the path followed by Barbados and other Caribbean countries. Lewis is aware of the dangers of excessive foreign capital. He hastens to suggest that Caribbean governments failed to use foreign capital to increase the rate of domestic saving to 20 percent of national income (CDB 1972:9). Lewis is therefore not condemning foreign capital *per se*, but the failure of Caribbean people to save more.

An important analysis made by Lewis (1955:351) is that protection of manufactures is indicated in the Lewis model because in labour surplus economies, the marginal product of labour in manufactured goods exceeds the marginal product in food production. In the subsistence sector, labour is paid more than its marginal product. It is socially profitable to transfer such labour to manufacturing as long as the productivity of this labour is positive. There is consequently a case for protectionism to expand the output of manufacturing. We have already noted that while Lewis's closed model supports increased manufacturing, this is not really at variance with increasing labour productivity in food.

My principal criticism of Lewis's work is the unequal income distribution that the closed model reinforces. This original model is not a normative model and gives no normative prescription for the distribution of income to the poor majority during the course of development. Lewis (1976) is aware of the inequality inherent in capitalist development. He assigns to government a crucial role in the redistribution of income either through the budget, land reform or other means. He concludes that a reduction in inequality does not necessarily imply a fall in the growth rate. Our analysis of the Barbadian case will show how it was necessary to use the budget as a redistribution instrument to offset the income inequality inherent in the capitalist development process (see Chapter 11).

LEWIS'S PUERTO RICAN MODEL

The Puerto Rican model was a policy model of development put forward for the English-speaking Caribbean by Lewis (1950). There is a close relationship between Lewis's conceptual framework and this policy model. The principal impetus for rapid industrialization was overpopulation on the land. Not only was agriculture unable to absorb the excess labour supplies, but technical progress was also reducing the actual numbers in agriculture. Excessive supplies of labour were also reflected in the hypertrophy of the tertiary sector, as manifested in the burgeoning of petty trades and domestic service in the 1950s.

In the colonial scenario it was necessary for the Caribbean islands to develop an export trade in manufacturing, while increasing agricultural productivity. Lewis argued that the region lacked experienced entrepreneurs skilled in export marketing. Metropolitan expertise was therefore essential to enable regional competition with existing suppliers. Further, it was assumed that the region was short of capital, thereby strengthening the case for the invitation of foreign capitalists. Fiscal incentives, combined with a relatively lower real wage, would entice foreign capitalists to invest in these countries.

The chief mechanism for the expansion of the Puerto Rican model was the increase in the rate of growth of the capitalist surplus at a relatively low real wage. The implied role of the state in this model was to cover social overheads in the field of public utilities and regulate private enterprises considered as substitutes for productive public enterprises. Further, the weakness of the indigenous capitalist class induced the state to pursue an open door policy towards foreign direct investment (FDI).

The Caribbean structuralist/dependency critique of the Puerto Rican model focused on the underdevelopment biases inherent in FDI. This argument maintained that Lewis underestimated the importance of the multinational corporations (MNCs), which repatriated their profits and undermined the sovereignty of the host country. Another variant of this view advanced by G.K. Lewis (1968) is that the Puerto Rican model was a form of neocolonialism, a thesis that states in part that the economic elites that comprised the Caribbean governments welcomed such a model because it increased cultural dependence on "higher" external societies.

Lloyd Best (1980) advanced an alternative "residentiary" model. Best argued that it was the "traditional" small-scale and labour-intensive sector and not the "modern" large-scale and capital-intensive sector that had been the source of dynamism. The Puerto Rican model was designed to promote expansion in the modern sector. Best posited the thesis that modernization should have led to expansion in the traditional or "residentiary" sector providing for the domestic market. Best's argument is theoretically flawed because it fails to make contact with the problem of surplus labour, which Lewis diagnosed in the 1950s. The existence of excess labour with possible zero marginal productivity could not have provided a dynamic market for rapid industrial growth based on home market expansion.

The view is tenable that, despite the failings of the Puerto Rican model, Lewis has been harshly and many times unfairly criticized. The Lewis strategy of export promotion industrialization can be regarded as pathbreaking in much the same way as the Prebisch case for industrialization in Latin America. Both Lewis and Prebisch reinterpreted the theory of comparative advantage. While Prebisch argued the case for protectionism of domestic industry, Lewis advanced the rationale for the promotion of labour-intensive manufactured exports in the context of regional integration. Theoretically, this thesis was valid in the context of the 1950s.

Lewis's Puerto Rican model has been criticized, not so much in terms of the arguments relating to the need for export-oriented industrialization, but in terms of the foreign investment strategy recommended to achieve that goal. Our view is that because of Lewis's adherence to modernization theory within the intellectual context of Caribbean societies of the 1950s, he regarded settler-type foreign investment as a faster route to development. It is argued here that some degree of direct foreign capital was necessary to finance imports and supplement domestic savings. However, the problem in the Caribbean became one of over-reliance on foreign capital. However, the post-colonial policy-makers should be faulted because the model in its initial stages placed too much emphasis on import-substitution, which did not generate the dynamics to reduce the dependence on FDI. Policy-makers also failed to harness, as a matter of urgency, local managerial skill and entrepreneurship. The slow development of the indigenous industrialist class perpetuated the dependence on foreign capital.

THE PLANTATION ECONOMY MODEL

This section provides a highly condensed outline of the plantation economy model. This model was advanced to explain underdevelopment features of the contemporary Caribbean economy. First, the domestic economy is structurally part of an "overseas economy". The latter comprises the "metropole", a locus of decision-making, and the "hinterland economy", a supplier of raw material to the metropole. The plantation in the hinterland is a "total economic institution". This second characteristic means that the plantation is a self-contained economic unit controlling its own production and distribution. The third feature, "incalculability", refers to the measure of price indeterminacy arising from the exchanges between the plantation and the metropole.

The five "rules of the game" constitute a mercantilist relationship between the metropole and the hinterland. The "*inter caetera* provision" defines exclusive spheres of influence of a metropole; the "muscovado bias" restricts the hinterland to terminal activity; the "metropolitan exchange standard" defines the monetary relation between the metropole and the hinterland; the "navigation provision" guarantees metropolitan intermediation in all hinterland trade; "imperial preference" defines the general provision under which producers in the hinterland dispose of their output in metropolitan markets. In this schema, the Caribbean economies were hinterlands of Great Britain. Best's notion of metropole and hinterland is synonymous with the centre/periphery dichotomy of the broad dependency theory.

The phase of the pure plantation economy (1600–1838) exhibited a staple cycle that can be divided into a foundation period, characterized by the acquisition of capital in the form of slaves and equipment. This trade was organized by the joint stock trading companies. The hinterland experienced a golden age when profits were high and slaves plentiful. However, this period was followed by maturity and decline as the soil became less productive, the cost of slave labour increased, and market demand in the metropole contracted.

The period of plantation economy modified (1838–1938) was initially characterized by labour shortage when the slaves were emancipated. The problem of labour shortage was addressed by the importation of indentured labour from India. During this phase, also, a peasantry attempted to establish itself, but the plantation continued to monopolize the best land. The emergence of a peasantry sharpened the conflict between staple and "residentiary" activity. The plantation economy modified remained structurally dependent despite the emergence of the peasantry.

The further modified phase of the plantation economy extends into the contemporary period and is characterized by new staples such as tourism and mining. The MNCs replicate the features of the old plantation system. The control of the modern MNCs over primary production, such as bauxite and oil, is tighter than that of the old merchant companies over the planters. Dependency persists and indigenous initiative is suppressed. The conflict between "residentiary" and staple activity is exacerbated as hinterland governments actively promote branch-plant type foreign investment. Lewis's Puerto Rican model epitomizes Best's notion of "plantation economy further modified".

The plantation economy model can be considered the cornerstone of Caribbean structuralist thought and a representative species of a large genus of structuralist dependency writing. This model provides a descriptive conceptual framework for examining the relationship between the metropole and hinterland. It is generally recognized in the literature that the model represents a typology rather than a theory of social change. The concept of plantation economy can be interpreted to convey the view that this relationship may continue even if the old plantation system is modified. Thus, resource allocation is distorted despite changes in the nature of the staple.

Plantation economy further modified continues to exhibit most of the rules of the game that Best identified. The "muscovado bias" still persists, in the sense that the processing and disposal of output (e.g., bauxite and sugar) are largely located in the metropole. The MNC has vertically integrated hinterland activity into the complex of metropolitan markets. The navigation provision remains because goods are still transported by metropolitan carriers of MNCs. The metropolitan exchange standard has been modified. Some CARICOM territories adopted fixed parities with the US dollar, and they have the autonomy to devalue their currency. Others have floating currencies. Further, central banks have introduced new flexibility into monetary management because of their ability to create money. Finally, imperial preference persisted for a large part of this period, but was modified as neoliberal arguments promoted the reduction or elimination of trade preferences.

Girvan's (1971a) insightful analysis of bauxite also illustrates clearly the persistence of Best's notion of incalculability in the pricing of bauxite. Vertical integration leads to transfers between subsidiaries in different countries. Girvan argues that this has introduced a high degree of incalculability in the pricing of bauxite and its products, and this leads to incalculability in the value of output and ultimately in the amount of profits made. As a result, the company can manipulate prices and therefore profits, consequently enabling it to minimize its tax obligations to the host governments. Transfer pricing is a feature of the operations of the MNCs.

Although most of the rules of the game remain intact, the nature of the dependency relationship has changed as a result of globalization. The MNC has introduced a new type of modernization. It has made available new technology as well as a new configuration of commodities and services. Further, the MNC has created new class divisions. Highly paid wage labourers in some sectors like bauxite coexist with relatively lowly paid workers in manufacturing. Local dependent managerial elites exist in MNC subsidiaries in banking and the insurance business. This new division of labour contrasts with the slave labour system and the tenancy arrangements after emancipation.

The rapid spread of modernization and globalization has created different types of macroeconomic problems related to deficit financing, balance-of-payments adjustment and higher levels of international indebtedness. It is contended that new macro models have to be developed to explain these changes. The Best model of plantation economy further modified, though identifying important institutional features of the contemporary economy, was not advanced to explain the short-run dynamics of the domestic economy in the context of the contemporary world economy. Specifically, the Best model never proposed to explain or to predict monetary and fiscal processes and other complexities of economic management in the post-1980 economies in the globalization era. Indeed, other aspects of the neoliberal approach, such as trade liberalization, deregulation and tax reform, cannot be explained by the Best model. These were characteristics of Barbadian development after 1990.

The plantation economy model has been criticized as an analytical construct. There is support for the view that the mechanisms of the Best model are not theoretical constructs but descriptive categories. Critiques by Sudama (1979), Bernal et al. (1984) and Benn (1974) all discuss the absence of socio-political and class analysis in the Best model. Though we can agree that the model lacks an interdisciplinary framework, that is, a political economy orientation, class struggle analysis is not inherently important to its operation. The model can be conceived as descriptive of underdevelopment rather than a theory of economic development.

POLICY RECOMMENDATIONS OF PLANTATION THEORISTS

This section discusses a broad set of policy recommendations suggested by plantation theorists, some of which were implemented by Barbadian policy-makers. These are compared with those of the Lewis model. Plantation theorists advanced a wide range of policy prescriptions, but these have not been developed into a rigorously specified operational model at the national level. Girvan (2002) argues that the original plantation model did not say much about the role of the state. Bernal et al. (1984) describe their policy reforms as a "programme". My analysis therefore attempts to document the various views of the plantation school, which included Best and Levitt, Beckford, Girvan and McIntyre. We can identify five major policy concerns: localization of decision making; the role of the state; diversification of the production structure; income distribution and regional integration. Our comparison between Lewis and the plantation theorists leans on Bernal et al. (1984) who present a roughly similar categorization.

Localization was proposed as the logical countermeasure to foreign domination. Plantation economists recommended the nationalization of plantations and foreign banks, as well as the mining industry (see Beckford 1972:220–228 and Girvan 1971b). Their "programme" also favoured the creation of indigenous banks. Further, McIntyre and Watson (1970) recommended that incentive legislation should have been used to discriminate in favour of national ownership, by varying the incentives granted to correspond with the degree of the local share in the equity. They recognized that changes in the pattern of ownership would not lead to instant transformation since the process also depended on developing adequate local personnel.

The theoretical argument for ownership and control had both micro- and macroeconomic implications. At the micro level, local ownership was encouraged to establish effective control over the pricing and marketing of commodities, as well as the purchasing and processing of raw material supplies. At the macro level, local ownership and control would arrest the outflow of the domestically generated economic surplus. As a welfare instrument, nationalization was also conceived as a means to redistribute income and wealth, particularly in the rural sectors of the economy dominated by foreign-owned plantations.

The tendency for establishing state-owned institutions to compete with foreign-owned MNCs was criticized by Thomas (1974) on the grounds that it led to duplication and waste. The local state-owned competitor model was also subject to careful scrutiny in the banking sector. Evidence advanced by Bourne (1974) showed that such duplication was possible, and an ideology of development based on localization is not a sufficient condition to trigger development in an economy dominated by profit-maximizing banks. Barbados showed some adherence to the localization model by the establishment of the Barbados National Bank.

Although the Lewis model accommodates state ownership, since capitalists can be local, foreign or state capitalists, a policy of nationalization (or localization) is not indicated in the Lewis model as a precondition for transformation. Our interpretation is that the role of the state in the Lewis model was to create a favourable environment for capitalist accumulation in the "modern" sector.

Plantation theorists therefore favoured some degree of state capitalism, as reflected in their recommendation to control "the commanding heights of the economy". Recently Girvan himself has admitted that "the advocates of statist policies (including myself) were unduly optimistic about the capacity of state-owned enterprises to be agents of economic transformation" (see Girvan 2002). Best also explicitly rejected imported Marxism. Best (1980) conceived the state as a vehicle for strengthening capitalism in what he called the "residentiary" sector of the economy. This distinction between "residentiary" expansion and "modern" sector expansion is the fundamental difference between Best and Lewis.

Both the Plantation School and Lewis assigned to the state a crucial role in short-term economic management to buttress the long-term development strategy. This concern was expressed by the Plantation economists following the devaluation of sterling in 1967, and by Lewis in his presidential address to the Board of Governors of the Caribbean Development Bank in 1972. The devaluation of sterling in 1967 raised questions relating to the appropriate exchange rate policy that Caribbean countries should follow, as well as the effects of devaluation on the income distribution and the need to redefine the goals of monetary management. Lewis was concerned, not only with the "overvaluation" of Caribbean currencies, but also the need for restraint on wage incomes to reduce domestic costs. To Lewis, wage control had to be accompanied by an active policy to improve the income distribution. These issues are important because a long-term development strategy in dependent Caribbean economies must be supported by an appropriate exchange rate strategy and restraint on the growth of wage incomes. The discussion of these issues, particularly in the annual Monetary Studies Conferences, has been the important legacy left by Lewis and the Plantation School.

Plantation theorists recommended diversification of the production structure to reduce dependence on staple production. This general strategy depended on the implementation of a number of policies at the sectoral level. These included increased agricultural production for the domestic market based on increased peasant output; the local processing of agricultural raw materials; the use of local materials in manufacturing and the forging of linkages between various sectors of the economy. These structural reforms closely followed those of the Latin American structuralist approach. These reforms at the local level were intended to be consistent with the goals of regional integration. Development planning in Barbados was informed by these strategies.

Whereas Lewis's argument for increased labour productivity in food was based on adverse terms of trade, Plantation theorists based their argument on the general underdevelopment biases of the plantation system. In this regard the Plantation theorists neglected the specific role of the factoral terms of trade as a factor conditioning development.

Plantation theorists regarded regional integration as the relevant development model. The enlargement of the market from regional integration would generate economies of scale as well as external economies for regional production. The theoretical arguments for integration were concretized in the establishment of CARICOM. Lewis also proposed regional integration for developing countries. However, he did not spell out in detail the various mechanisms of regional integration in the Caribbean. Economists of the Plantation School, such as Thomas, Brewster and McIntyre, have contributed significantly in this area. The contribution of Demas should also be mentioned here.

The need for income redistribution is indicated in the plantation economy model because the plantation system generates inequality. Land reform was recommended as an instrument of income redistribution. Beckford (1972:223) favoured a redistribution of the best lands to the peasants. However, the income redistribution analysis lacked rigour, which might be partly explained by the sparse data on income distribution in the 1960s. The Lewis model was based on a distribution in favour of capitalists, but Lewis (1976) was aware of the need for redistribution to the poorer classes.

A brief summary is now in order. Plantation economy theorists recommended partial closure of the economy to reduce foreign domination. Strategies of localization, nationalization and regional integration were integral parts of this schema. They neglected other concerns, such as the terms of trade and the importance of outward-looking development. Their contribution was nonetheless important, because it led to a new awareness of the need for some degree of self-reliance and national consciousness. Lewis differed from the Plantation School in the sense that he advanced a model of development rather than underdevelopment. An operational export-oriented model, rather than a "programme" of policy reforms supported his development theory. This assessment realizes the worth of the ideas of both Lewis and the Plantation theorists in analysing the complex realities of Caribbean development. Our analysis in this book will show how Caribbean structuralism, embodied in the work of Lewis and the Plantation theorists, influenced policy making and development in Barbados.

SIZE AND PLANTATION ECONOMY

The historical/institutional/structural methodology of the plantation economy model does not explain why some countries, for geographical reasons, are more likely to be chronically dependent. However, the physical size/dependency thesis is not mutually incompatible with this model. Size as a parameter merely reinforces some of the features associated with Best's notion of plantation economy further modified. According to Brookfield (1979), small size explains largely why the staple economy remained locked into an offshore-producer relationship in spite of changes in the nature of staple activity. The size constraint, therefore, can be incorporated theoretically into a historical study of the national economy. Further, the size constraint supports the export orientation of Lewis's policy model, since it defines physical and economic limits on the expansion of the domestic goods and capital market.

The theoretical contribution of Demas (1965) was to relate the physical concept of size to dependence and the process of "structural transformation". The importance of his thesis is its indication that size limits the range of policy options available to small countries and is therefore a binding constraint on the rate of structural transformation. Demas is prepared to analyse the size parameter while abstracting from historical and institutional variables. Even though he is aware of these factors, his argument is that size provides the structural context and is unalterable. Size also generates structural dependence.

Demas's central position is really derived from the classical thesis that economies of scale are limited by the size of the market. The size constraint is an important consideration not only in manufacturing, but also in administration, public utilities and some kinds of services such as education and health. Lewis also understood the importance of size when he recommended export promotion industrialization to overcome the limitations of the domestic market. Although population size is not the only variable affecting the size of the market, it defines the physical upper limit for the expansion of the domestic market. Further, scale constraints affect the growth of the domestic capital market. The small capital market is characterized by a narrow range of financial instruments, which imposes restrictions on the mobilization of internal finance for development. The theoretical implication is that the small economy will depend on capital inflows.

Scale constraints stemming from the small size of domestic markets limit the internal range of backward and forward linkages. Linkages effects are generated outside the geographical confines of the economy because the small size of the domestic market orients the economy towards exports in order to realize the benefits of economies of scale. The highly skewed resource base implies that the economy will rely heavily on imports of intermediate goods and raw materials. The high import coefficients in the small economy also result from the divergence between the narrowly based structure of production and domestic demand. The physical size constraint also implies that the small country will not be able to generate its own endogenous growth dynamic because its capital goods sector is likely to be very small or nonexistent. The absence of a capital goods sector will considerably limit the gains to be derived from import substitution industrialization. Demas's analysis rationalized the urgent need for policies to promote regional integration and influenced theoretical investigations in this area.

The physical size approach of Demas has shed some light on the constraints on development in the typical staple economy. However, the concept of size as a purely physical phenomenon needs some modification, because some physically large economies display similar behavioural patterns. We identify two dimensions of size, namely, size as a purely physical phenomenon and size as a purely theoretical construct. Prachouny (1975) views size as a theoretical abstraction with no physical properties. He argues that a small open economy is any country that treats the price of any internationally traded good or asset as exogenously determined, and aims to maximize some objective function, given this constraint. The relevant line of inquiry is whether a country can be regarded as "small" and hence dependent, if it can treat variables such as the foreign interest rate, import and export prices, the level of capital inflows and exchange rates, *inter alia*, as exogenous variables. The contention is valid that if a country cannot determine any of these variables by its own domestic activities, then that country should be considered theoretically "small". However, there is a strong relationship between small physical size and small theoretical size. That is, the physically small economy, by reason of its structural constraints, is by necessity a price taker. The two dimensions of size are relevant to our conceptualization of the Barbadian economy after 1946 and help us to understand the persistence of certain structural and historical problems in the contemporary period.

A fundamental deficiency of the Demas thesis of physically small economy, however, is that it does not place enough emphasis on the role of management in the national economy of the small system. Given the invariance of the structural constraints, it is contended that the orientation of development policy and the management of allocation and distribution are significant determinants of the character of the small country's development path. The policies of the state and the efficiency of their implementation can impact on certain institutions, technology and human resources and can therefore cause an outward shift in the production possibility frontier. The ideologies adopted by Caribbean governments after 1960 are also important considerations explaining the different development outcomes in these countries. The views of Best (1971) and Blackman (1979) have some validity. They argue that a small country has some "room to manoeuvre". The resource allocation process in a small dependent system is partly a function of development policy and management.

SUMMARY

The conceptual issues discussed in this chapter provide an analytical frame of reference for empirical work on Barbados's economy. Lewis's theoretical framework is logically consistent with the operational Puerto Rican model discussed later in Chapters 3 and 6. The emphasis on income distribution in the theoretical model suggests some discussion of the actual distribution under the Puerto Rican model. The theoretical model also suggests an investigation of credit financing of capital formation, as well as the mobilization of voluntary and involuntary domestic savings.

The plantation economy model is the relevant theoretical framework for understanding the persistence of certain institutional and structural phenomena in Barbados. These include the dichotomy between plantation and peasant agriculture; the survival of imperial preference and the "muscovado bias" in the sugar industry. The persistence of the rules of the game is analysed in relation to the rise and fall of sugar after 1946. The performance of sugar during the early survey period is closely reminiscent of the Best/Levitt "staple cycle". The emergence of the new tourism staple is typical of plantation economy further modified.

The nature of the transition process can now be summarized briefly. In Barbados colonialism provided the initial conditions that led to the emergence of the corporate plantation system and the pattern of trade and resource allocation in the period before and immediately after World War II. Small economic size provided the structural context that reinforced the economic tendencies inherited from the colonial past, as well as imposed operational constraints on the implementation of development policies. After 1990 the Lewis and Best models lost some of their explanatory power as the Barbadian economy became further integrated into the world economy through market liberalization and globalization.

3

Colonial Development Policy and Planning

COLONIAL DEVELOPMENT POLICY

Colonial development policy informed the development planning strategy immediately after World War II. In Chapter 1, we inferred that British colonial policy just before the end of World War II rested on two principles. First, Britain conceived her changed relationship with the colonies as one of "responsible trusteeship", rather than one based on the extraction of surplus. Second, in the opinion of the Colonial Office, the colonies had a comparative advantage in the production of primary products. The principle of comparative advantage was the model that informed colonial development and is the focus of our present discussion.

The comparative advantage thesis dominated the documents produced by the Colonial Office during the 1940s. However, there is some evidence to support the view that even though primary production was of paramount importance, the Colonial Office encouraged some measure of industrial development, at least in principle. But there was considerable ambivalence in the proposals for industry, as shown in the important Benham and Gallotti reports discussed below.[1] These reports underlined the comparative advantage principle while paying lip service to restrictive forms of industrialization.

During World War II, the British colonies had attained a measure of self-sufficiency in certain types of manufacturing output. Towards the end of the war, the Colonial Office observed that industrial development in the British colonies should be allowed to continue if agriculture was unable to solve the problem of unemployment due partly to rural–urban migration. This position was reiterated immediately after the war:

> The colonies ... are primarily agricultural and they must continue to rely on agricultural production ... for their main source of national wealth. This does not, however, mean that the total income of particular colonies cannot be enhanced by the improvement of existing industries or by the introduction of new ones. (Colonial Office 1947a:90)

The metropolitan position was that the private sector should carry the burden of any industrial development. It was considered that such industries should not be dependent on state aid, and the Colonial Development and Welfare (CD and W) grants generally reflected this principle. The emerging IMF also cautioned about the heavy cost involved in industrialization, and stressed that the greatest improvement of the well-being of people in the colonies should come from increasing their productivity in agriculture (IMF 1950:25).

Visiting economists such as Benham echoed this metropolitan policy stance, which was reflected in the crystallization of the "development planning idea" during this period. The Benham Report is the embodiment of the neocolonialist thesis. Although its focus was on Jamaica, its findings theoretically were applicable to other colonies. The Benham Report viewed colonial man as unproductive, a perception supporting the opinion that this was a salient cause of underemployment. The report was not in favour of promoting "infant" industries (except for a category called "safeguarded" industries) by raising protective duties. Such duties inflated the price of locally produced goods relative to imported goods, thereby reducing the standard of living. The Benham Report was convinced that further industrialization would make very little contribution towards solving the employment problem. The safeguarded industries would prevent dumping of products by overseas manufacturers. Benham's heavily circumscribed industrial programme supports Brett's (1973) view that the Colonial Office was not in favour of an industrial strategy in the colonies that would significantly reduce the colonies' imports of British manufactured goods.

The neocolonialist ideas implicit in Benham's analysis were mirrored in the pessimism of Gallotti. The latter was of the opinion that industrialization as a solution to Caribbean unemployment was severely limited, on theoretical and practical grounds. Theoretically, the net impact of industrialization was to increase unemployment and imports generally. Gallotti asserted:

> The new and expanded industries do undoubtedly provide a certain amount of work and pay out a considerable sum in wages; equally evident they reduce the imports of certain goods. But the net effect may nevertheless be to intensify the problems of unemployment and unbalanced trade. (Colonial Office 1948:13)

Gallotti's thesis was that industrial progress leads to a rise in imports, which stimulates living standards and population growth, and hence creates an imbalance between the rate of growth of the labour force and the labour absorption capacity of industry.

Metropolitan industrial growth was not a good example for the colonies. Gallotti submitted that, although the high per capita incomes in the metropole were no doubt associated with the expansion of secondary industry, this was attributable to high labour productivity and continuous development of techniques and skills. In the West Indies, however, "it may well be easier and more profitable to improve the technique and equipment of agriculture than to foster sound manufacturing industries" (Colonial Office 1948:15).

Emerging from our contextual analysis is the interpretation that neo-colonialism based on the principle of comparative advantage was enshrined in the colonial reports as well as the Moyne, Benham and Gallotti reports. The neomercantilist thesis was central to colonial development planning. In this context, the industrialization model of Lewis represented a critique of neomercantilism by stressing the essential complementarity that existed between industry and agriculture. It is now appropriate to pursue an empirical analysis of the colonial planning strategy.

COLONIAL DEVELOPMENT PLANNING

The Barbadian planning experience was conditioned largely by important internal and external political developments. The internal decolonization process in Barbados after World War II was determined by changes in British colonial policy and by the Third World decolonization movement. A policy of gradual decolonization aided the formulation and implementation of development plans after 1946, by giving elected members of parliament more direct control in the legislative, executive and administrative affairs of the colony. The change in the character of the state that made this control possible was the transition from a semi-ministerial system of government in 1946 to full ministerial status in 1954 and internal self-government in 1961. Prior to 1954 real control of decision making was in the hands of the colonial governor. Sir Grantley Adams, the premier of Barbados, played an important role in the decolonization movement. The attainment of political independence in 1966, under the leadership of Prime Minister Errol Barrow, gave the state new autonomy in the conduct of its external affairs, thereby facilitating the inflow of foreign capital necessary to finance the development plans.

Long-term plans for welfare and development in the British colonies were recognized as early as 1940 and were an integral part of the operations of the 1940 Colonial Development and Welfare Act.[2] However, at that time there was not much insistence on the obligation of colonial governments to contribute to the cost of carrying out their own development plans. Further, the 1940 act had only allocated grants totalling £5 million to the colonial empire to cover ten years. The 1945 Colonial Development and Welfare Act increased this grant to £120 million and made greater insistence on the formulation of development plans (see Howard 1989:22). Development planning was based on the policy of expecting each territory to utilize its local resources. Further, each territory was asked to estimate how much it could afford to earmark for development projects from its surplus balances, loans and general taxation.

The early plans, between 1946 and 1960, were basically descriptive documents with a listing of public sector projects. Colonial development planning in Barbados was geared toward the financing of "social overheads", especially toward the end of the 1950s, but there were no explicit policies of structural change and income distribution articulated in these plans. Apart from the emphasis on infrastructural development, the state's policy was limited to supporting private capital, particularly in agriculture. The economy remained largely underdeveloped, with a highly skewed income distribution.

Steve Emtage (1969) argued that there were two principal constraints on planning in colonial Barbados. The first was constitutional, and the other related to the question of size and economic dependence. As Emtage observed, even if one accepts the view that Barbados's colonial status imposed some limitations on the use of domestic policy instruments, this constraint cannot explain the unwillingness of the colonial government to implement strategies to bring greater equity to the socio-economic structure. Emtage asserted that the metropolitan power was even willing to countenance some degree of direct governmental intervention. Both road transport and the distribution of natural gas were nationalized and this involved shifts in the ownership of assets and the balance of economic power. But such intervention cannot be regarded as a fundamental departure from colonial policy. The colonies remained committed to the principle of British responsible trusteeship and agrarian capitalism.

Early planning was devoted heavily to the finance of sugar monoculture and to the services supporting the sugar industry. It was hoped that such expansion of sugar would be based on a scheme of consolidation of factories, which would lead to economies of scale as well as increased opportunities for the development of by-products. Development of better irrigation facilities and improvements in the public water supply would assist in broadening the basis of agriculture. The 1946–56 plan allocated a mere £50,000 to industrial development, to be utilized in exploring the possibilities of and developing minor industries. Similarly, tourism received £10,000 (Howard 1989:24).

To sum up, the development plans of the 1950s were merely extensions of colonial budgeting to include the planning of capital expenditure. Most of the plans were financed by revenue surpluses and general taxation, as well as by CD and W grants. The major change in the 1955–60 plan was the shift to loan financing of capital expenditure, particularly foreign borrowing, which became a feature of post-colonial planning. Foreign loans and CD and W grants accounted for 42.2 percent of total planned expenditure. The increased reliance on external financing reflected the transition from colonial rule to internal self-government and political independence.

POLICY AND PLANNING IN THE SERVICE ECONOMY PERIOD

Planning in Barbados during the service economy period continued to be public sector oriented. The analysis here deals with the public policy aspects of planning and, to a lesser extent, the financial implications of planning. Development planning was primarily concerned with statements of intended projects for the public sector. Additionally, the development plans provided the major policy statements on the promotion of foreign investment in the pursuit of import substitution and export promotion strategies. However, the plans did not involve comprehensive structural or indicative planning of non-public sector activities.

Another significant feature of post-colonial planning was the heavier emphasis on foreign borrowing to finance development. This borrowing was mainly from international development agencies, such as the World Bank and Inter-American Development Bank. Financing from revenue surpluses gradually became less important, particularly after 1973 when the government was able to pursue deficit financing by borrowing from the central bank. My discussion now looks at the public policy foundations of post-colonial planning.

Planning during the 1960s was concerned with the implementation of Lewis's Puerto Rican model (1950). This model argued that fiscal incentives, combined with a relatively low real wage, would encourage foreign capitalists to invest in manufacturing industry in the Caribbean. The planning strategy proposed direct foreign investment along import-replacement lines, and comprehensive legislation to support such investment. A high level of protectionism was enshrined in the Industrial Incentives Act of 1963, which granted to eligible manufacturers a ten-year exemption from customs duties on imports used in production. The promotion of foreign capital was based partly on the inability of the local capitalist class to promote industrialization. The Barbados Development Board was the chief instrument of industrial planning during this period.

The initial difficulties of industrialization in a small developing economy quickly became apparent. Subsequent plans posited that the basic reason for the continuing unemployment was that manpower resources had outpaced resources of land and capital. At the same time, however, the increased levels of capital allocated to the sugar industry, as well as export industries, had reduced employment possibilities. Further, the policy initiatives in manufacturing and tourism did not bring about a corresponding reduction in unemployment. The perceived limitations of the strategy of import replacement prompted the state to adopt a strategy of export-promotion industrialization. It was recognized that because the domestic market was small in size and purchasing power, the possibilities of import substitution on a large scale were limited, and heavy reliance had to be placed on industries producing for the export market.

Despite this adherence to the foreign investment model, planning during the late 1960s showed a departure from previous plans in terms of limited direct participation of the state in agro-industry, agricultural marketing, and the hotel industry, that is, in areas normally considered the preserve of the private sector. The establishment of the Pine Hill Dairy in 1966, as well as the Agricultural Development Corporation in 1965, was intended to provide institutional support for agricultural diversification. The Barbados government was a major shareholder in the dairy, the duty of which was to provide a variety of milk products for local consumption. The Agricultural Development Corporation was designed to stimulate and encourage the development of agriculture in the private sector and to manage government-owned estates and agricultural projects on a commercial basis.

The new role of the state as a limited entrepreneur was seen in the construction of the Hilton Hotel, which was estimated to cost $7.63 million and was intended to provide direct employment for between 225 and 250 people. Direct government participation was limited to two-thirds of gross operating profits, while the remaining one-third accrued to Hilton Hotels International for management services. However, as we have seen, this limited form of state ownership was not accompanied by broad localization or nationalization policies, as was the case in other Caribbean countries, like Guyana and Trinidad.

During the 1970–85 period, the Barbadian planners attempted to specify the nature of the development problem and modify the planning strategy in light of the initial post-war experience with foreign investment. The development plans during this phase acknowledged the importance of greater national participation in the economy. Greater emphasis was also placed on the provision of public goods and infrastructure by way of project planning.

Local entrepreneurship had to be stimulated. For the first time, the heavy dependence on foreign capital became a measure of concern. According to the 1969–72 plan, foreign capital had financed about 30 percent of gross fixed capital formation in the period 1956–59, compared with 70 percent in the period 1960–64. As much of this capital was in the form of equity, the magnitude of future outflows of factor incomes was important. As the plan stated, efforts to diversify the structure of production had been accompanied by an almost total reliance on foreign capital, with the result that one form of structural dependence was in danger of being substituted for another.

Despite more than a decade of factory industrialization, the structural rigidity, persistent structural unemployment, and growing balance-of-trade deficit remained major problems. It was necessary to utilize domestic resources more effectively and increase the participation of nationals in key sectors of the economy. The new emphasis on local capital was especially important in the context of the tourism industry. While the participation of foreign capital had been responsible for the rapid expansion of accommodation, and while the continued inflow of such capital was welcomed, the government considered that there should have been increased local investment in the tourism sector of the economy. It was hoped that local entrepreneurship and national productivity would be stimulated through the Barbados Hotel School and the Barbados Institute of Management and Productivity (BIMAP). The latter institution was proposed in 1969 and established in 1972. Further, the national orientation of the 1969–72 plan was reflected in the stated goals of the Barbados Development Bank. This bank was founded specifically to mobilize domestic resources to finance local entrepreneurs. Shares of the bank were available for public subscription, to facilitate and encourage saving and investment.

The national participation objective was also a theme of the 1973–77 plan, which expressed the hope that greater self-sufficiency in economic performance would be achieved. But there was some ambivalence about adoption of policies to increase self-reliance. The policy-makers were concerned about the extent to which an economy historically dependent on external sources could quickly shift to indigenous sources without endangering existing standards of living. In fact, the official attitude toward self-reliance was nebulous and unsatisfactory. The 1973–77 plan called the development of a greater degree of self-sufficiency in the economy a process of seeking adjustment of social, political and economic values at some satisfaction point between autarky and dependency.

Apart from paying lip service to self-sufficiency, Barbadian planners after 1970 made a new and definite commitment to export promotion industrialization as a major plank of the development strategy. It was proposed that during the 1970s, "enclave" industries would provide the major impetus in the export strategy. An export promotion agency was to be instituted in 1974 to undertake market research. The agency would play a major role in providing information on export credit finance and insurance. Enclave industrialization provided new jobs, particularly for women, but most of the jobs had a low skill content, with the exception of certain areas of electronics requiring engineering skills.

However, the most important feature of development planning after 1973 was heavy public sector spending financed largely by foreign borrowing. The 1973–77 plan projected that foreign borrowing would finance Bds $91.7 million, or 52.2 percent of capital expenditure over the planning period. Further, the massive public investment programme of 1979–83 was supported by substantial foreign financing, totalling Bds $239.1 million, or 42.6 percent of capital expenditure, a commitment that was quite large compared with that of previous years. Policy-makers between 1973 and 1990 were convinced that the weakness of the manufacturing and tourism sectors, consequent upon the impact of the 1973 oil price hike, required heavy investment by the state in the economy to maintain levels of employment.

The plans between 1977 and 2000 did not depart from the philosophies of earlier plans. There was a heavy emphasis on sectoral planning, comprising a listing of sectoral objectives and strategies. After 1990, the Barbadian government's enthusiasm for development planning seemed to have diminished. In 2000 Sir Courtney Blackman, former governor of the Central Bank of Barbados, was commissioned to write a strategic plan for Barbados (see Blackman 2001). There is no evidence that the Barbadian government ever implemented Blackman's plan, although policy-makers remained committed to the idea of a strategic plan for Barbados.

DEFICIENCIES OF PLANNING

Although the essence of development planning is good public policy, we can identify some of the technical deficiencies of the planning process after 1960. Development planning in Barbados during this era was strongly politically oriented and was characterized by a tendency to concentrate on socially desirable projects with a strong appeal to the electorate. Although the implementation of projects consequent on this emphasis was an important means of providing employment and public goods, the policy-makers tended to pay less attention to "structural planning". Thus, the post-war plans did not create the sectoral linkage effects fundamental for the development process. Although this deficiency was excusable in the rudimentary stages of planning in the 1950s, the later plans should be faulted for not paying attention to the linkage aspects of development.

A more serious defect of post-war planning, however, was that most of the plans minimized the importance of technical manpower planning. One of the most binding constraints on development was the shortage of skilled manpower. This constraint was critical in the construction industry during the 1980s. Manpower planning ought to be an integral part of development planning and should take account of labour force mobility, migration, transport problems, attitudes about various types of work, relative wage rates, and factors affecting productivity. There is no evidence that manpower requirements were well projected in order to identify critical shortages of skills in the various sectors of the economy.

Another limitation of the post-war plans is that forecasting techniques were usually rudimentary or nonexistent. For example, in the plans of the

1980s there was no analysis of the impact of the large capital works programs on the monetary base or the balance of payments. This arose from the fact that the plans were not seriously concerned with forecasting the demand for imports. There is no evidence of attempts to incorporate input-output analysis in the plans, even on a preliminary basis. Although quantitative planning has limitations when applied to small, open economies, there is still a need to develop such techniques, not as substitutes for qualitative analysis, but as aids in decision making.

The introduction of an energy plan was a commendable feature of the 1979–83 plan. However, planning for the development of energy resources should not merely be a statement of policy. The planner must analyse the relationship between energy and development by calculating energy intensity ratios (ratios of energy consumption to output) in various sectors. This approach to the analysis of energy efficiency should be combined with regression analysis to forecast the demand for electricity and gasoline. Such forecasting enables the planner to measure precisely the impact of tourism, manufacturing and the household sector on the balance of payments. In sum, more time should be devoted to planning development, rather than simply to writing a development plan.

However well it is done, planning in small economies is a difficult and frustrating exercise. Demas (1965) identified four fundamental limitations to overall planning in West Indian economies. These were high levels of openness, the relatively small role played by the public sector, dependence on foreign capital and the dominance of MNCs. Only three of these limitations are now important, as the public sector is now much larger than it was in the 1960s and cannot be considered a constraint on planning. The high level of openness means that the difficulty of predicting foreign sales is a primary constraint on planning. Openness also implies that significant cost overruns will be encountered in the planning of projects, as a result of unforeseen increases in import prices, particularly the price of petroleum.

Foreign investment and the presence of MNCs also posed problems for plan implementation and projections. Enough care was not taken by Barbadian planners in projecting the level of outflows of profits and dividends from these economies. Further, domestic tax revenues were overestimated because of the difficulty of calculating the tax loss arising from transfer pricing employed by multinational firms. These difficulties partly explain why the Barbadian planning experience did not achieve a high level of success after 1960. Many of the plans were poorly implemented.

SUMMARY

This chapter has analysed the evolution of development policy and planning in Barbados after 1946. Colonial development policy was influenced predominantly by the British approach to development and welfare in the colonies. Considerable emphasis was placed on agricultural development and the provision of social infrastructure. The British colonial perspective was that industrialization should not be the leading economic strategy in the colonies, because Britain wanted to protect manufacturing industry at home.

The foreign investment strategy informed development policy after 1960. The basis of the strategy was state-aided industrialization. The incentive-aided foreign investment aspect of the policy was extended to the tourism industry. At the same time the post-colonial state actively increased its provision of public goods, made possible as a result of higher levels of foreign borrowing. Considerable time and attention were devoted to the writing of development plans, which were really programmes for the public sector.

After 1970 the policy strategy became more service oriented. Tourism was regarded as a leading sector and this was supported by the active pursuit of enclave industrialization and offshore financial business. Energy conservation and the search for new energy sources occupied policy-makers after 1973 following the first "oil shock". Nevertheless, despite shifts in the basic model, the policy strategy during the period reflected the state's continued dependence on foreign capital. Sectoral planning characterized the planning approach between the late 1970s and 2000. Although development planning was not very successful, the macroeconomic management of the economy was efficient for most years of the service economy period. The next chapter discusses the process of structural change and growth.

4

Evolution of the Macroeconomy

STRUCTURAL CHANGE

The development policies discussed in the previous chapter diversified the Barbadian economy away from sugar production. Before examining the dynamics of the leading sectors of the economy, it is necessary to outline the pattern of structural change. My analytical framework hinges on a division of the economy into three broad sectors – primary, secondary and the tertiary or service sector. The national accounting data, though non-comparable in the early post-war period, help us to discern broad trends and structural shifts over time.

The earliest and most substantial attempts to depict the size and structure of the Barbadian economy on a time series basis were carried out by Bonnett (1956) and the Barbados Statistical Service (1960). This early work shows the overriding importance of primary production during the period 1946–64. These sources reveal that primary output averaged roughly 46 percent of gross domestic product (GDP) between 1946 and 1956. The other sector of importance during this period was the tertiary or service sector. The hypertrophy of the service sector reflected disguised unemployment. A large part of this sector would correspond to Lewis's subsistence sector dominated by domestic service and petty trades (see Lewis 1954). The heavy emphasis on the distributive trades was largely a consequence of the trade orientation of the economy. Service-oriented activities averaged around 37 percent of GDP during this period. Secondary output, which averaged 17 percent of GDP, comprised mainly sugar factory operations, but cottage industries such as dressmaking, tailoring and the potteries were also significant.

The structural analysis for the years 1955–64 utilized work by Bethel (1960) and the Barbados Statistical Service (1960). The estimates support the view that the primary sector, though still strong, was declining between 1955 and 1960. The service sector became larger as the economy became more monetized and the distributive trades increased in importance. By 1960 the primary sector contributed 28.1 percent to GDP, the secondary sector (including sugar manufacturing) 18.1 percent and the service sector 53.8 percent (see Table 4.1).

Table 4.1
Sectoral Distribution of GDP (Selected Years; Percent)

Sector	1955	1960	1970	1980	1986	1990	2000
Sugar	23.4	21.3	9.9	6.4	2.8	2.0	1.5
Other agriculture	11.8	6.8	4.8	3.4	3.6	3.4	3.0
Mining	–	–	–	0.8	1.3	0.7	0.7
Manufacturing	19.8	8.3	10.1	10.9	9.8	8.0	6.3
Transport and public utilities	6.2	5.7	7.6	7.5	12.3	11.3	13.6
Construction	7.3	9.8	10.1	7.2	5.6	6.5	5.8
Distribution	10.6	23.0	26.0	21.8	20.9	20.0	17.6
Tourism	–	–	–	12.0	10.0	11.4	11.3
Other services	12.2	15.3	15.9	15.1	17.4	18.2	22.7
Government services	8.7	9.8	15.6	14.9	16.3	18.5	17.5
Total	100.0	100.0	100.0	100.0	100.0	100.0	100.0

Source: Barbados Statistical Service and Central Bank of Barbados, *Annual Statistical Digest* (2002).

One can observe a further decline in the primary sector from around the early 1960s and a compositional change in the output of the secondary and service sectors. Services played an increasingly important role as a contributor to the GDP after 1960, rising from 53.8 percent of GDP in 1960 to 82.7 percent in 2000. This expansion of the service economy is explained largely by the increased participation of the state in the economy after 1960, the growth of tourism and banking, and the expansion of external trade and distribution. The compositional shift in tertiary output was also reflected in the relative decline in petty trades and domestic service. Indeed, the strong growth of service activities mirrored the increased structural dependence of the economy after 1960. An important point is that the secondary manufacturing sector never became the leading sector in the Barbadian economy after 1960, even though the composition of manufacturing production shifted from cottage-based commodities to factory output. The contribution of the new manufacturing sector to the GDP rose from around 8.3 percent in 1960 to 9.8 percent in 1986 and thereafter declined to 6.3 percent in 2000.

Disaggregated GDP ratios are presented in Table 4.1 to facilitate our analysis of specific output trends in the economy. The following trends are obvious:

1. A rapid decline in the ratio of sugar output to GDP after 1960;
2. A decline in the contribution of other agriculture;
3. A gentle rise in the contribution of manufacturing after 1960, but a decline after 1980;

4. As early as 1960, the distributive trades replaced sugar as the most important contributor to the GDP;
5. The rapid expansion of the government sector, and the strong performance of other services, such as finance and business services towards the end of the survey period;
6. The overall buoyancy of the services sector.

AGGREGATE DEMAND

It is appropriate to discuss changes in the structure of aggregate demand. Our analysis is severely limited by a gap in expenditure data between 1964 and 1974. Private consumption expenditure averaged around 75 percent for the colonial period 1946–60. The high level of consumption expenditure in the early post-war period was functionally related to labour income from primary production. The buoyancy of the sugar industry led to an increase in labour incomes and consumption after the war. Bonnett (1956:256) notes that "about half the increase in labour incomes from 1949–1951 accrued to sugar industry workers, while half of the increase from 1951 to 1953 was enjoyed by service workers".

The dependence on sugar incomes and the low level of economic development also explain the consumption patterns of lower income groups during this period. Previous work by Bonnett (1956:237), Cumper (1960) and Straw (1953) suggests that a high proportion of income was spent on food. This observation is interesting, though not surprising during the early stages of development. According to Bonnett, expenditure on food averaged 52.9 percent between 1949 and 1953. Bonnett's work was based on Straw's budget survey of 1951 and 1952, which found that households spent an average of 56 percent on food. Cumper's analysis points to the expected inelasticity of food expenditures during this period.

Despite the absence of data for the period 1965–73, we can still hypothesize on the behaviour of consumption during this period. Following the well-known thesis advanced by Chenery (1960), structural changes induced by import substitutive industrialization and tourism in Barbados augmented intermediate and final demand. We may also expect the proportion of income spent on food to decline, following Engel's law. However, institutional changes in the demand for durable consumption goods also played an important role. For example, the introduction of easy hire-purchase arrangements as early as 1957 permitted consumers to purchase a large number of consumer durables. The growth of the commercial banking industry in the 1960s and 1970s also had the effect of stimulating expenditures on imported consumer durables. The ratio of private consumption expenditure to GDP was 72 percent in 1980 but fell to 67.2 percent in 2000 (see Table 4.2).

Table 4.2
Expenditure on GDP (Selected Years), Percent Distribution

Category	1980	1985	1990	1995	2000
Private consumption expenditure	72.0	76.9	63.6	61.5	67.2
Government consumption expenditure	15.6	18.9	20.2	20.0	18.2
Gross capital formation	23.5	15.4	18.8	15.1	18.3
Exports of goods and services	65.4	67.7	49.1	58.2	49.8
Imports of goods and services	76.1	60.0	51.7	55.0	56.3

Source: Central Bank of Barbados, *Annual Statistical Digest* (2002).

Capital formation during the early post-war years was concentrated in the areas of building and construction. Investment behaviour, particularly between 1956 and 1964, was largely attributable to the rapid growth of government capital formation. Indeed, this was especially so in 1957 and 1958, when around $20 million were spent on the construction of a new deep-water harbour and improvements to the airport. However, the growth of consumption outstripped the growth of capital formation during the early 1960s. Between 1964 and 1974 there was considerable construction activity in the hotel industry, which stimulated growth in private fixed capital formation. There was a declining investment ratio immediately after 1974 stemming from the oil crisis of 1973 and the depression in the international economy. Private investment slowed down and many government projects were shelved, particularly in 1975. For instance, the ratio of gross domestic capital formation to GDP fell from 24.1 percent in 1974 to 19.2 percent in 1975.

The philosophy of increased state activity, alluded to in the previous chapter and developed in later chapters, influenced the behaviour of investment after 1975. Development policy designed to increase infrastructure led to a sharp rise in the investment ratio from 19.2 percent in 1975 to 27.4 percent in 1981. The years just before 1981 marked a period of expansionary expenditure policy. The philosophy of increased state activity became dominant because the Puerto Rican model was unable to fulfil employment goals, and was not very resilient to external shocks in the world economy, particularly the oil shock of 1973 and the world recession of 1981.

Boamah (1996:47) states that investment after 1981 fell in response to declining profitability in the tourism sector. This partly explains the decline in the investment ratio after 1980. Additionally, the recessionary period of 1991–93, discussed in Chapter 12, led to a further decline in the investment ratio.

Boamah's (1996) data also showed that the ratio of gross domestic savings to GDP peaked at 21.4 percent for the period 1976–80, coinciding

Table 4.3
Savings and Investment Ratios in CARICOM Countries

Country	Gross Domestic Savings as % of GDP (1997–99)	Gross Domestic Investment as % of GDP (1997–99)
Bahamas	–	–
Barbados	14.9	18.3
Guyana	32.3	41.2
Trinidad and Tobago	27.9	28.5
Jamaica	–	–
Belize	15.9	24.0
Antigua and Barbuda	29.1	42.9
Dominica	–	–
Grenada	14.4	38.5
Montserrat	(27.5)	59.8
St Kitts and Nevis	23.7	41.1
St Lucia	17.6	25.4
St Vincent and the Grenadines	8.0	30.0

Source: Caribbean Development Bank, *Annual Report* (2000).

with the highest investment ratio. The savings ratio continued to fall thereafter, reaching a level of 14.9 percent for the period 1997–99. Table 4.3 shows that Barbados's savings ratio is low when compared with other Caribbean countries. Subsequent chapters present data on foreign capital in various sectors of the economy.

BARBADOS'S GROWTH PERFORMANCE

This section describes the growth of the Barbadian economy between 1966 and 2000.[1] The statistics for this period are much more reliable for assessing the real growth of the economy. A study by Craigwell and Lewis (1998) attributes most of this growth to the impact of capital formation and labour. It is estimated that the Barbadian economy grew at a real growth rate of 5.7 percent per annum between 1966 and 1971.[2] These years immediately after independence were characterized by a stable world economy and expansion in most sectors of the Barbadian economy. The 400 percent oil price increase disrupted this pattern of growth in 1973–74, and the growth rate of the economy declined as a result of a combination of rampant inflation, reaching 38.9 percent in 1974, and a fall in real output.

The economy recovered between 1975 and 1980. During this period real output increased at an annual average rate of 5.2 percent. This was due to increased momentum in the export sectors and augmented government spending. This period of recovery was interrupted by the 1980

Table 4.4
Some Macroeconomic Indicators 1986–2000

Indicator	1986	1991	1995	2000
GDP per capita ('000)	8.9	11.1	12.0	16.0
Real growth (%)	5.1	(3.9)	2.3	3.1
Inflation (%)	1.3	14.6	3.9	3.1
Unemployment (%)	17.7	17.3	19.6	9.2

Source: Central Bank of Barbados, *Annual Statistical Digests*.

oil price increases and a sharp recession in the world economy. These two factors placed considerable pressure on the balance of payments. Foreign debt service as a ratio of the exports of goods and services rose from 3.3 percent in 1981 to 7.2 percemt in 1985 (Barbados Ministry of Finance 1987:86).

Recessionary conditions continued in the economy up to 1985. Unemployment rose sharply from 10.8 percent in 1981 to 18.7 percent in 1985. Annual real growth rates remained low or negative. The average annual rate of growth for the period 1981–85 was –2.6 percent. The government went to the IMF in 1982 to secure a standby arrangement of eighteen months duration.[3] It was only in 1986 that real GDP grew again by 5 percent as a result of sharp tax cuts and heavy government spending. The economy went into recession again in 1991 when real output fell by 3.9 percent. Table 4.4 gives some major indicators on the economy between 1986 and 2000. Particularly important is the high level of unemployment recorded before 2000. I return to some of these points in Chapters 9 and 12, since they are related intimately to other aspects of development.

INCOME INEQUALITY

The following critique advances the view that income inequality was determined primarily by the ownership structure of the colonial economy. Further, despite structural changes under the Puerto Rican model, a sizeable proportion of the labour force continued to live on subsistence incomes. It is difficult to make definitive statements about the changing income distribution in Barbados, because the severe paucity of reliable budget studies does not allow a meaningful statistical investigation of income distribution over the entire period. We examined income inequality by choosing representative samples of primary and secondary data for the period of colonial development (1946–60) and the service economy period (1960–91). It is hoped that this critique will provide a reasonable picture of income inequality during the period.

The institutional structure of colonial society suggests that income inequality was functionally related to underdevelopment and the concentration of wealth in the hands of the merchant class and the plantocracy. The problem was one of asset distribution. The existence of a merchant class comprising a few wealthy families, along with a high level of disguised unemployment, were primary determinants of income inequality in the services sector. Similarly, the size of farm holdings was inextricably linked to inequality in the distribution of income and wealth in the agricultural sector. This is due to the fact that by 1961, a few large farms in the estate sector, constituting about 3 percent of total farms, owned over 70 percent of the total acreage.

The pattern of income distribution associated with institutional inequality was shown in Straw's (1953 and 1954) studies of budgetary patterns in the colonial economy. Straw's analysis shows a highly skewed distribution. His work was based on household surveys conducted in 1951 and 1952. Straw found that average incomes were lower in the rural areas, but in the "crop" season incomes in the richest agricultural zones were higher than in the urban areas. Second, in "hard times" 78 percent of the households received an income of less than twenty dollars per week, while 43 percent got less than ten dollars per week. In the crop season the proportions were 66 percent and 30 percent, respectively. Third, at the lower end of the income scale, some 63 percent of households with an average income of below fifteen dollars received 30 percent of the total incomes accruing to households in hard times. In the crop season the proportions were 49 percent and 19 percent, respectively.

Subsequently, analyses by Cox (1978) and Holder and Prescod (1984) reached the conclusion that there was an overall decrease in income inequality during certain years of the service economy period. Their findings were based on the use of the Gini coefficient: a coefficient approaching unity shows a high level of inequality, whereas a coefficient approaching zero reflects an improvement in the income distribution. Cox found a Gini coefficient of 0.426 for 1970 and 0.404 for 1974, indicating that the distribution of income in 1974 was less unequal than in 1970. Cox reported that there was a worsening in inequality for lower-income groups in 1974 and an improvement for middle-income groups. He stated that the improvement for middle-income groups outweighed the increase in inequality in the lower ranges, making the overall inequality less than in 1970. Cox's analysis suffered from the fact that the Lorenz curves intersected. Methodologically, intersecting Lorenz curves cannot show whether the overall distribution improved. As a result, Cox's interpretation is incorrect.

Holder and Prescod (1984), using a methodology similar to that of Cox, point to the decline in overall income inequality as shown by the fall in the Gini coefficient over time from 0.455 in 1960 to 0.345 in 1980.

A later work by Boamah et al. (2003), using the same income tax methodology, reported a post-tax Gini coefficient of 0.589 for 1999. Our work avoids a duplication of this analysis, using income tax data to measure inequality in a developing country characterized by over 60 percent of workers who do not pay income tax. Our approach evaluates critically the results of the unpublished studies by Cox, Holder and Prescod, as well as Boamah et al., to provide a better perspective on the level of inequality in Barbados.

The following critique moves from the general to the specific. The limitations of income tax data for income inequality analysis related to the problem of under-reporting of income and under-enumeration of income recipients. There is also the difficulty of measuring net income from subsistence farmers. Again, not all income recipients are required to file a tax form. This is particularly so at the bottom of the income distribution.

More specifically, the 1970 analysis by Cox suffered because taxable returns constituted only 36 percent of the labour force, leading to the view that a high level of income was under-reported. The Holder and Prescod approach is subject to an even more severe criticism. The Annual Financial Statement and Budgetary Proposals for 1980 indicated that 30,000 people in the labour force were no longer liable to pay tax with effect from that income year. Therefore, the observed fall in the Gini coefficient to 0.350 in 1980 obtained by Holder and Prescod did not take account of the 29 percent of the labour force at the bottom. Their findings reflected an improvement in the income distribution of middle-income taxpayers who submitted tax returns, rather than the income distribution of the economy as a whole. The rise in inequality reported by Boamah et al. (2003) is a measure of the distribution of disposable income of those taxpayers who submitted tax returns.

It is also reasonable to argue that the purchasing power of lower-income groups may have declined during the period 1970–77, attributable, *inter alia*, to the impact of rising unemployment levels. The years 1973–77 were characterized by stagflationary conditions of the "oil crisis" of international capitalism, which slowed the rate of growth of real output. Unemployment rose from 9.7 percent of the labour force in 1970 to 15.7 percent in 1977, thereby expanding the numbers in the zero income bracket, many of whom were previously employed in the manufacturing sector.

The analysis of income inequality during the service economy period is buttressed by household budget data for the period April 1978 to March 1979 provided by the Barbados Statistical Service. These data show that 26 percent of the households sampled received a monthly income of less than $200 ($50 per week), while 54.3 percent of households received less than $500. At the top of the scale, 2.8 percent of households received a monthly income of over $2,000 per month. If this sample is an indication of the

larger population it means that there were still marginal income dispari-
ties under the Puerto Rican model. Using the same data, Downes (1987)
found a Gini coefficient of 0.4638 for disposable income.

The inequality problem is not only a problem of nominal income
distribution but also a problem of the asset distribution in the society. We
note that Downes's statistical analysis of the income distribution data is
technically correct. However, I have conceptual difficulties with his conclusion, made on the basis of the Gini coefficient, that income inequality
increased between 1951–52 and 1978–79. Even though a rise in inequality
is possible, the Barbadian economy had undergone structural changes as
well as changes in the asset distribution. To make comparisons over such
a long period of time requires data on the wealth or asset distribution,
which may not be readily available. Second, in the post-independence
economy, the majority of people had greater access to secondary education, low-cost housing, better health care, transfer payments and social
services such as family planning, national insurance and social security.

I am aware of one study on income distribution and poverty in Barbados for the 1990s. Diez de Medina (1997) found a Gini coefficient of
0.41 in 1996, which meant an improvement in the income distribution,
since it was closer to zero than Downes's (1987) 0.4638. Diez de Medina
(1997) also estimated a per capita poverty line for Barbados of Bds $5,290
(US $2,645) per annum. This was done on the basis of the estimation of
an annual food basket, which measured minimum nutritional requirements, and valued these requirements using the minimum costs of different items. The food basket was augmented by a non-food component
not explained in his study. He found that 12.7 percent of total households,
or 20 percent of the population, lived below the poverty line.

Our discussion has illustrated some of the difficulties of measuring
the true income distribution in an open developing economy. As the Lewis
model shows, the nominal income distribution can worsen and real wages
fall during the capitalist development process. This is so because diver-
gences are likely to arise between private profitability and social costs
during development, as well as terms of trade deterioration. Therefore,
the task of the state is to ensure that the welfare of poorer sections of the
community is maintained by guaranteeing access to low-cost housing,
adequate sanitation, free education, health and community services,
which would compensate for any decline in real wages resulting from
terms of trade deterioration. It is also contended that measures such as
Gini coefficients should be interpreted with great caution in developing
countries. Such coefficients are useful when data are accurate and available for all income groups. But very often these measures do not capture
the high degree of inequality at the bottom end of the income scale, since
subsistence incomes in both the rural and urban sectors are usually under-
reported.

During the 1990s, "social indicator" or "quality of life" approaches, such as the Human Development Index (HDI) and the Human Poverty Index (HPI), supplemented the money income distribution approach to the inequality problem. The HDI is a measure of a country's standard of living developed by the United Nations Development Programme (UNDP). The index comprises three components: education, income and life expectancy at birth. The HDI lies between zero and one, and countries with high levels of development have an HDI above 0.8. These comprise mainly European countries. Barbados, with an index of 0.888, was ranked at number 27 in 2001, and was therefore the most developed of the developing countries. The HPI is a broad measure of poverty and focuses on four dimensions, namely, longevity, knowledge, economic provisioning and social inclusion.

THE DISTRIBUTION OF ECONOMIC POWER

Very little is known empirically of the wealth distribution in Barbados. There is a strong view in contemporary Barbadian society that wealth and economic power are still heavily concentrated in the hands of the white mercantile class. Karch (1979) and Barrow and Greene (1979) have examined the entrenchment of the white agro-commercial elite in Barbados from around the mid-1800s. Barrow and Greene recognized that knowledge of the quantitative character of elite ownership is difficult to estimate precisely. They examined the network of directorships in the 1970s and suggest that white ownership and control were particularly strong in the distributive sector of the economy. At the same time Barrow and Greene (1979) identified the persistence of what they called "black dispossession", another term for the landless poor.

The issues of race, economic ownership and wealth distribution came to a head in the 1986 Barbadian general elections. Karch (1997) observed that black economic "powerlessness" became the focal point of daily radio talk shows. The Bussa Committee in 1987 coined the term "economic democracy" (Karch 1997:298). This committee was established to stimulate discussions on black marginalization in the corporate sector in the late 1980s. The debate on racial issues resulted in the so-called Mutual Affair in 1988, an issue arising out of the financial activities of the Barbados Mutual Life Assurance Society (BMLAS). Beckles (1989) was the first writer to highlight this issue.

Beckles (1989, 2004) discussed the process by which many blacks were excluded from the leadership of the white-dominated corporate sector. Beckles (2004) contends that the BMLAS was a symbol of white financial power, and that the historical evidence showed that the BMLAS had functioned for over 100 years as a leading financial bastion against blacks in Barbados. The BMLAS achieved this by representing certain interest groups in the white corporate sector at the expense of most policyholders. According to Beckles (2004), the "Mutual Affair" of 1988 emerged when black policyholders became interested in sitting on the board of directors of the BMLAS in order to manage their capital controlled by whites. The "Mutual Affair" was therefore the national crisis that brought to the fore the issue of "economic democracy".

Although the white commercial elite has survived in the corporate sector, this sector has experienced some diversification and growth, thereby broadening the base of share ownership. However, many lower- and middle-income Barbadians are still reluctant to buy shares because of the perception of the risks involved. Another constraint on the growth of share ownership is that firms are more dependent on loan capital than share capital. Wood (1998) explains that this is due to the relative ease of borrowing from commercial banks, as well as the reluctance of many firms to dilute family and closed circle ownership and the control of business.

PRICES AND WAGES

No attempt is made here to pursue a detailed analysis of price and wage determination in Barbados. I refer the reader to studies by Downes, Holder and Leon (1990), Cumberbatch (1997) and Downes, Holder and Leon (1991). The inflation research suggests the strong conclusion that the import price level was the most important determinant of the domestic price level. The evidence does not suggest that demand inflation, generated by money creation, is significant in the Barbadian context. Downes and McClean (1982), Boamah (1985) and Mascoll (1985) have carried out further work on the behaviour of wages.

An important consideration is the role played by wages in the development process. To what extent did wages in the non-agricultural sectors induce workers away from the agricultural sector in the 1960s and 1970s? The sharpest decline in labour employed in agriculture in the entire survey period occurred between 1958 and 1975 (see Chapter 5). We therefore examined firm data between 1960 and 1976 to gauge the differences between the average weekly wages in agriculture compared with the non-agricultural sectors. Table 4.5 shows that the level of average weekly wages in the non-agricultural sectors was higher than in agriculture. This phenomenon partly explains the fall in the supply of labour in agriculture during the 1960s and 1970s. Mascoll (1985) found that although agriculture registered high labour productivity growth, this sector registered a slow growth in real wages. For the economy as a whole the rate of productivity growth was higher than the rate of growth of real wages. I was unable to find data on average weekly wages for the 1980s and 1990s to compare with the data presented in Table 4.5. However, the wage index published by the Central Bank of Barbados, *Annual Statistical Digest* (2002),

Table 4.5
Sectoral Distribution of Average Weekly Wages (Selected Years; $)

	1960	1963	1966	1969	1972	1976
Non-agricultural sector	25.8	27.0	31.5	38.3	48.4	95.8
Agricultural sector						
(a) Males	–	–	21.6	25.3	39.9	76.7
(b) Females	–	–	17.5	18.8	25.5	48.2
Manufacturing	23.1	26.2	31.5	37.3	49.5	98.5
Transport	18.0	30.0	35.0	45.0	68.0	125.5
Mining and quarrying	–	–	30.0	33.0	57.5	89.0

Source: International Labour Organization, *Yearbook of Statistics* (1966, 1979, 1978).

shows that the rate of growth of wages in agriculture after 1980 was much slower than that for other sectors such as distribution, transport, construction, public utilities and manufacturing. See also Chapter 5 for other factors causing the decline in the agricultural workforce.

In terms of the determination of the rate of growth of wages, work by Downes and McClean (1982) suggested the important role of trade union aggressiveness, and import and export prices. In an open economy such as Barbados, the rate of inflation is a strong determinant of the wage rate.

5

Agriculture

INTRODUCTION

Agriculture plays a vital role in the development process as an employer of labour. Agriculture also provides food for an expanding population, as well as resources for capital formation. In the Barbadian economy, the export bias in agriculture has been important in providing foreign exchange for capital formation in other sectors. At the same time, local food supplies have not kept pace with the growth in domestic demand for agricultural commodities. While the dependence on sugar has paid dividends in terms of its foreign exchange and development contribution, this export bias has created other problems for the diversification of domestic agriculture.

This chapter therefore has a dual purpose. My first intention is to demonstrate how certain institutional features of the agrarian system reinforced the dependence on sugar exports. I also examine the problems facing sugar in the contemporary period. However, it is argued that the performance of agriculture cannot be explained solely with reference to the dependency thesis. Certain policy-induced structural changes in the economy, as well as competition for land, affected resource allocation in the primary sector. My second objective is to outline the constraints facing crop diversification, including the competition from other sectors of the economy for resources such as labour and land.

EARLY CHANGES IN THE AGRARIAN STRUCTURE

It is appropriate to discuss the agrarian structure between 1946 and 1971. Sufficient data were not available to examine the agrarian structure in the 1980s and 1990s. However, many of the patterns identified in the past continue up to this day. The Barbadian agrarian structure has been characterized by great inequality in the size distribution of farm holdings. This inequality demonstrates the sharp dichotomy between the corporate plantation (sugar estate) sector and the peasant (small farm) sector. The censuses show the high degree of fragmentation of small farms after World War II.[1] In 1946, 86 percent of all farm holdings were between one and five acres. The 1946 Census of Agriculture did not report on holdings under one acre or "holdings without land". The figures for 1961 and 1971 are more comparable. The Census of Agriculture for 1961 revealed that holdings of fewer than five acres were 65 percent of total holdings. By 1971 this figure had fallen to 47.8 percent, because many small farmers had holdings without land, indicating the rapid fragmentation of the peasant sector. Further, those farmers owning fewer than five acres controlled 13.3 percent of the total farm acreage in 1961 and 11.7 percent in 1971. In contrast to the pattern of fragmented peasant holdings, some 170 farms in the category "over 200" acres, representing 3.4 percent of the total number of farms, controlled 75.6 percent of the total farm acreage in 1946. This small group in the sugar estate sector controlled 73.8 percent and 77.5 percent of total acreage in 1961 and 1971, respectively.

The size distribution of farms has implications for dependency, income inequality and resource allocation processes. Most farms up to this day cultivate sugar cane, although a large quantity of agricultural land has been used for real estate after 1980. Peasant holdings are usually confined to poorer soils, leading to relatively lower crop yields than those of the estate sector. Most smallholders allocate their land to sugar cane because of better marketing possibilities for this crop. Further, sugar cane cultivation does not require the same level of care that is needed for vegetable and root crop cultivation. This emphasis on sugar cultivation, however, cannot guarantee enough income to support a family and forces the smallholder to depend on the plantation for employment. Moreover, the small crop yields on peasant land do not ensure economies of scale in sugar cane growing. Many of these views were expressed by Farley (1964), henceforth known as the Farley Commission, which was of the opinion that the considerable fragmentation of the small farm sector led to a suboptimal utilization of land.

Historically, the estate sector is dependent on sugar. This sector has always enjoyed a good relationship with the commercial sector in terms of the marketing of sugar. Primarily because of the export orientation of the estate sector and its disinclination to cultivate crops other than sugar, agricultural supply does not adjust to domestic agricultural demand. The hypothesis that the size distribution of farms and dependence on sugar leads to distortions in the pattern of land resources use in the primary sector is subject to empirical verification.

An important feature of the agrarian structure in Barbados for the entire survey period is the predominant local ownership of land.[2] We choose to emphasize this phenomenon because it contrasts with the type of ownership structure analysed by Beckford (1969) where MNCs dominate plantation production and incomes are channelled into the metropolitan economy. The sole implication of local ownership is that the bulk of the income from sugar exports accrued to the residents in the domestic economy. However, structural dependence is persistent primarily because the export orientation of both the local corporate plantation ownership and small farm sector implies that a large part of income has to be spent on imported food and other goods and services. Although the Farley Commission attributed this pattern of dependence mainly to the economic marriage between the estate and commercial sectors, it can be argued that the export bias is not principally an outgrowth of ownership. The export of sugar has always been regarded by both plantations and peasants as a rewarding activity for institutional and marketing reasons.

The land tenancy system is also important. The plantation system was characterized by large land holdings operated by hired managers. The Census of Agriculture for 1946 and 1961 both revealed these ownership patterns. The analysis shows that farms occupying 66.4 percent of the total land area in 1964 were operated by managers, while 72.6 percent of farms over 100 acres were managed. Similarly, the managed acreage as a proportion of the total arable acreage was 74.9 percent in 1961. The McGregor Report (1979) also estimated that the proportion of managed arable land in Barbados was 86.2 percent in 1979. On the other hand, most land in the peasant sector is owner-cultivated. While the Farley Commission and the McGregor Report have cited absentee ownership in the plantation sector as a factor retarding rural development, one needs to examine the whole question of the utilization of resources in the agricultural sector rather than over-emphasize the land tenancy argument.

The question of efficient resources allocation in agriculture relates not only to land tenancy but additionally to a wide range of factors, including the quality of the land, capital and technical knowledge, marketing arrangements, infrastructural support and so forth. Beckford (1968) and Brewster and Thomas (1967) have argued that there is an inverse correlation between farm size and the degree of land utilization. Their argument implies that peasant lands are more efficiently utilized than estate lands.

Adequate data are not available to measure the efficiency of total resource use in the small farm sector. Beckford's contention that plantations underutilize resources should be examined in the context of structural change in the Barbadian primary sector. As we argue later, the decline in sugar production and increased production costs in the industry led to a rise in idle sugar lands after 1970, particularly in marginal areas. Some sugar estates were forced to sell real estate to realize their capital assets. Prior to 1971, the Barbadian evidence does not show a marked underutilization of arable estate land. In fact, agriculture censuses show that over 80 percent of the farm land of larger estates was under cultivation between 1946 and 1971.[3] The Beckford, Brewster and Thomas hypothesis, though verifiable for some Caribbean territories, is not strictly applicable to the specific case of Barbados.

Our final remarks on the agrarian structure relate to the high degree of concentration of farmland in sugar cane. The percentage of farms under sugar rose as the acreage per farm increased. For example, the proportion varied between 98 percent and 100 percent in the size group between 100 and 500 acres. In 1961, the percentage of total farms under sugar appeared to decline somewhat (to 72.6 percent), but this is explained by the inclusion of a group holding land between zero and one acre. Otherwise, the percentage of farms under sugar increased for all other size groups. By 1971, there was an absolute fall in the total number of farms as well as the percentage of farms engaged in growing sugar cane (68.3 percent). The 1971 data indicate, however, that the percentage of the total acreage under sugar was quite high, especially for farms over 100 acres. For example, farms of 100 to 200 acres held 89.1 percent of their land under sugar cane while farms over 500 acres cultivated the crop on all of their land. In 1971, land under sugar accounted for 94 percent of total acreage in farms. A survey of the economic fortunes of the sugar industry since 1946 follows.

THE RESURGENCE AND DECLINE OF SUGAR (1946–80)

This section analyses the "staple cycle" resurgence of sugar under colonial development, as well as its decline between the early 1960s and the late 1970s. The ratio of sugar exports to domestic exports averaged well over 70 percent in the 1950s, and the available estimates also show that the contribution of sugar to the GDP was in the region of 30 percent during the 1950s. In Chapter 1 we alluded to the social and class factors underlying the dominance of the sugar industry after World War II. It is appropriate to analyse other specific economic and non-economic variables that reinforced monoculture in the early post-war Barbadian economy.

The first noteworthy feature is the sharp increase in the sugar acreage reaped between 1946 and 1965. There was an increase of 10,000 acres of sugar reaped during this period. This was accompanied by an improvement in the yield of sugar as demonstrated by an expansion in the tonnage of cane per acre and yield in sugar per acre. Sugar production rose from 134,000 tons in 1946 to a high of 205,000 in 1957. This remarkable performance of sugar in the 1950s has been attributed partly to improved methods of husbandry as well as better varieties. Additionally, the 1950s was a period of particularly high rainfall that averaged well over sixty inches per annum. There was also a substantial increase in the application of imported fertilizer used mainly for sugar production. Also, technological advances in the industry increased economies of scale and improved overall production possibilities (see McKenzie 1958).

The extensive use of fertilizer and foreign technology stimulated growth but increased the import dependence of the sugar industry. Between 1950 and 1962, imported materials as a ratio of total materials used in the sugar industry averaged 64.3 percent. However, a caveat is

Table 5.1
Performance of the Sugar Industry

Year	Area Reaped (Hectares '000)	Canes per Hectare (Tonnes)	Sugar per Hectare (Tonnes)	Sugar Produced (Tonnes '000)
1961	19.8	70.7	8.2	163.0
1963	18.6	91.9	10.4	194.0
1965	20.2	87.1	9.9	199.0
1967	21.0	88.3	9.7	204.0
1970	20.1	72.3	7.7	155.0
1973	18.7	55.5	6.3	116.0
1975	16.1	52.5	6.1	98.6
1978	15.8	56.7	6.6	104.1
1980	16.1	74.9	8.5	136.6
1983	14.1	50.1	5.9	82.8
1985	13.9	57.3	7.2	100.2
1990	10.5	57.8	6.6	69.3
1995	7.5	47.6	5.2	38.8
2000	8.7	62.1	6.7	58.4

Source: Central Bank of Barbados, *Annual Statistical Digest* (2002).

important here. Estimates by Armstrong et al. (1974) show that for 1968 imported inputs in sugar cane growing were lower than those in other sectors of the economy. Imported direct primary inputs as a proportion of final demand were 7 percent for sugar cane cultivation, compared with 46 percent of final demand in construction, 37 percent in manufacturing, 45 percent for other agriculture and 27 percent in the hotel industry. The import component of sugar is lower than in tourism because in the latter industry leakages occur in the importation of food, construction materials, petroleum imports, expatriation of profits and so forth. Further, the local value added in sugar production is likely to be higher than for other import substitutive industries that are heavily dependent on imported raw materials.

The buoyant period of the 1950s and early 1960s was followed by a sharp decline of sugar in the late 1960s and 1970s. Hectares of sugar reaped declined from around 21,000 in 1967 to 15,800 in 1978 (see Table 5.1). The quantity of sugar production during the same period fell from 204,000 tonnes to 104,100 tonnes. There was also a marked contraction in the yield of sugar. The tonnage of canes per hectare dropped from 88,000 tonnes in 1967 to 56,700 tonnes in 1978, and the tonnage of sugar per hectare was down from 9.7 tonnes in 1967 to 6.6 tonnes in 1978. Sugar output continued to fall in the 1980s and 1990s, and by the year 2000, the hectares reaped were 8,700 and output was 58,400 tonnes. This sharp decline of sugar was associated with structural changes elsewhere in the economy and changes in resource use in the primary sector. The salient explanations of the deterioration of the sugar industry are as follows:

1. Removal of land from sugar cultivation;
2. Decline in the permanent labour force in agriculture;
3. High production costs in sugar;
4. Non-economic factors, such as poor rainfall and the burning of canes;
5. A fall in smallholder production.

The decline of sugar since the mid-1960s is associated with an overall change in land resource use in Barbados. There was a sharp fall of 12,175 acres of arable land between 1966 and 1976. Most of this land was previously under sugar. There was also a notable increase of 17,424 acres of land classified as "urban" during the same period (see Codrington 1978). This drastic change in land resource use was partly a result of the government's policy, which permitted the subdivision and sale of several plantations into two-acre lots. Other sugar cane lands were allocated for industrial and tourism development during this period. Furthermore, there was a rapid increase in land speculation. For an analysis of these subdivisions see Nurse (1979) and Barbados Sugar Producers' Association (1972:1).

Equally significant was the contraction in the permanent labour force in agriculture. Employment on estates declined from 17,700 in 1958 to 4,000 thousand in 1975. Factory employment also fell from 1,436 in 1958 to 555 in 1975. The growing labour shortage is attributable to supply and demand conditions that affect agriculture in the process of structural change. On the supply side, labour was attracted to employment in non-agricultural pursuits. This phenomenon is partly explained by higher wage levels in the non-agricultural sector, as well as the historically determined aversion to plantation work. Subsequent analysis in Chapter 8 indicates that emigration also reduced the number of people working on the land. The demand for agriculture labour was lessened by the diminished size of the sugar crop. Additionally, technological improvements reduced the demand for certain types of unskilled labour in the sugar industry. As a result of the interplay of these variables, the sugar industry became characterized by an aging labour force. The highest percentage of labourers in the sugar industry was in the group aged between forty-five and sixty-five years (Smith 1976:130). Labour scarcity often delayed the start of the harvest and contributed to time lags in getting canes to the factories. The processing of sugar was significantly slowed by labour shortage.

An additional factor influencing the decline of sugar before 1980, especially its profitability, was the high cost of production. According to

Persaud (1973) the 1961 cost of producing a ton of sugar was $176.16 compared to $203 per ton for 1968, resulting in a narrowing of profit margins. Part of the reason for the fall in profitability during this period was the drop in the world price of sugar from a peak of $372.28 per ton in 1963 to $85.12 per ton in 1968. Estimates for the 1970s show that the cost of sugar production was high, leading in some years to net losses. For example, according to Phillips (1977), production costs of sugar increased by 14 percent between 1970 and 1976. Despite the rise in the world price of sugar from $165.32 in 1970 to $1,343.50 per ton in 1974, profitability levels continued to be squeezed, as Barbados sold only about a quarter of its sugar on the world market. The high cost of production precipitated a marked decline in the financial viability of the sugar industry during the 1970s.

Other non-economic factors analysed in the McGregor Report also hastened the decline of the sugar industry. Average rainfall after 1960 was much lower than during the period of the 1950s. Poor rainfall was combined with an increased incidence of cane fires, particularly after 1965. These factors not only affected estate production but smallholders suffered adversely as well. In 1969 smallholders produced 15 percent of the canes milled. By 1974 this proportion had fallen to 12.76 percent (see Barbados Sugar Producers' Association 1974:1). Smallholders have also suffered from inadequate cultivation service and the absence of harvesting facilities, especially for the loading and transport of canes.

SUGAR IN FINANCIAL CRISIS AND DECAY (1980–2000)

The story of the sugar industry in the 1980s was that of an industry in the throes of financial crisis. As production and price levels fell, the industry continued to record heavy deficits. In 1982 the government provided the industry with its first financial support by guaranteeing a $17 million bond issue by the Barbados Sugar Factories Limited to finance a support price of $925 per ton of sugar for the 1982 crop. Part of the proceeds of local sugar sales was placed in a sinking fund for the redemption of the bonds.

The government also financed another $10 million bond issue by the Barbados Sugar Factories Limited for the 1983 crop. The purpose of these supports was to prevent the financial collapse of the industry. However, these initial financial props created new liabilities for sugar growers, and the continued depressed conditions of the industry meant increased dependence on the government for finance. Financial assistance to the industry in 1985 by the government in respect of losses on the 1984 crop was $15 million.

Continued high production costs and low prices led to heavy accumulation of debt by sugar plantations. By 1986 the contribution of sugar to the GDP had fallen to a mere 2.8 percent. The sugar industry never recovered in the 1990s, and by the year 2000 its contribution to GDP was 1.5 percent. See Table 4.1 for the contribution of sugar relative to other sectors of the economy.

IMPERIAL PREFERENCE

Imperial preferences reflected the survival of one of Best's "rules of the game", thereby perpetuating economic dependence. The primary focus of this section is on the two important sugar policy arrangements after World War II: the Commonwealth Sugar Agreement of 1951 and the Lomé Convention of 1974, which was renewed in 1979. These two agreements sheltered the sugar industry from market risks and to a large extent acted as a brake on the diversification of primary output. Such dependence also restricted the development of an economic strategy of structural change in the 1950s.

The Commonwealth Sugar Agreement of 1951 guaranteed a secure market for the export of sugar to the United Kingdom by Commonwealth sugar producers. Besides annually negotiated prices, the agreement provided for specific export quotas. The Overall Agreement Quota (OAQ) was the maximum amount a producer could export annually. The Negotiated Price Quota (NPQ) was the part of the OAQ for which the negotiated price would be paid. The difference in quantity between OAQ and NPQ was sold to preferential markets in the United Kingdom and Canada (see Persaud 1973 and *Barbados Sugar Industry Review*, no. 4 [September 1979]).

The Commonwealth Sugar Agreement was designed to guarantee a price that was "reasonably remunerative to efficient procedures". Between 1950 and 1964, price determination was carried out on the basis of the production costs of the producers. After 1965 there was greater scope for bargaining even on non-economic grounds, thereby weakening the principle that price increases would accrue to efficient producers. Although these price arrangements guaranteed an annual inflow of foreign exchange earnings from sugar, they provided no incentive for the high-cost producers in the Caribbean to rationalize sugar production to reduce the level of operating costs.[4]

The Lomé Convention of 1974 also buttressed the sugar industry in Barbados and elsewhere in the Caribbean.[5] The specific protocol relating to sugar ensured that the European Economic Community (EEC) undertook to purchase 1.4 million metric tons of sugar from the forty-six negotiating countries in Africa, the Caribbean and the Pacific (ACP countries). Barbados's quota was 49,300 metric tons, a reduction from the level obtaining under the EEC market at prices "freely negotiated between buyers and sellers", and the EEC intervened to purchase at the guaranteed price only where this price could not be obtained on the market.[6]

The neo-Marxist position on the Lomé Convention was unrealistic. The Lomé Convention was considered by some neo-Marxist writers as the consolidation of "neo-colonialism". According to Nabudere (1976), the Lomé Convention was a manifestation of "neo-colonialism" because it reproduced the production relations that existed under direct colonialism. In the Caribbean Gonzales (1976) argued that the Lomé Convention did not strengthen the political will to diversify. I disagree with this view, even though the Lomé Convention was premised on the maintenance of the flow of raw materials to Europe. High-cost producers in Barbados cannot survive by selling sugar on the world market. After 1990 the rationalization of domestic non-sugar agriculture, as well as the promotion of services, appeared to be the most pragmatic approach towards compensating for the weakness of Barbadian sugar as an internationally traded commodity.

POLICY AND PROBLEMS OF DIVERSIFICATION

The purpose of this discussion is to show that there was a limited degree of crop diversification in the agricultural sector. However, the non-sugar subsector remained relatively small and also declined during the 1970s. A consequence of this decline was that the economy continued to depend heavily on imported food. Non-sugar agriculture contributed 9.9 percent to the GDP in 1950, 6.3 percent in 1965, 4.2 percent in 1977 and by 2000 the figure had fallen to 3.0 percent. The analysis looks first at diversification during the period of colonial development.

Diversification of agriculture became a goal of economic policy during World War II, when limited export and import opportunities made concentration on local food production necessary.[7] Persaud and Persaud (1968) have shown that there was no progress in crop diversification between 1946 and 1965. Their argument is based on the fact that the acreage under food crops actually declined between 1946 and 1965: on inspected estates, the acreage planted in food crops declined from 11,000 acres in 1946 to 6,900 acres in 1965 (Barbados Statistical Service 1965:47). One general explanation of this decline is that colonial development did not have the diversification of the primary sector as a major objective.

Persaud and Persaud (1968) have analysed the specific problems of diversification in the period before 1965. They argue that the research and agricultural knowledge needed for vegetable and root crop production were in short supply. This type of farming requires a greater level of supervision and daily attention. Primarily because of the high level of perishability of these crops, marketing problems were much more acute than in the case of sugar. The part-time farming tradition in the small farm sector also militated against food crop production. Small farms seemed unsuitable for diversification because they occupied the drier areas with poorer soils. Persaud and Persaud (1968) also argued that the shortage of underground water in some parts of the island restricted the development of these enterprises.

The state became more committed to a policy of diversification after 1960. The *Barbados Development Plan* 1969–72 expressed government's intention to "maintain and if possible increase agricultural export earnings from sugar and develop exports of other agricultural commodities" (Barbados Government 1969–72:66). While government was studying diversification possibilities, the Barbados Sugar Producers' Association set up its own diversification unit in 1965. The aim of the unit was to study root crops that might supplement foreign exchange earnings from sugar. The principal export crop identified was sea island cotton. Successful trials with this crop led to its cultivation on a commercial scale by the Agricultural Development Corporation. The West Indies Sea Island Cotton Association was revived in the 1960s and obtained assistance from the British government, which supplied cotton harvesters for experimentation.[8]

Sea island cotton had been cultivated in Barbados in commercial quantities prior to 1946. Production fell sharply from 106,584 pounds of lint in 1940 to 12,552 pounds in 1948 as a result of the ravages of the boll weevil, as well as rising costs. When cotton was fully reintroduced in 1969, production rose to a peak of 352,000 pounds in 1975 but then fell off significantly to 58,571 pounds by 1977.[9] Some of the problems encountered in the growing of cotton were labour shortages as well as the unwillingness of private farmers to plant this crop during the period following the high sugar prices of 1975.[10] During the 1960s cotton production fluctuated, reaching 277,587 pounds by 1986. The government's search for new export crops to supplement sugar also led to experiments with onions, which became an important export crop during the 1970s.

The data on non-sugar agriculture after 1970 allow us to assess the performance of this subsector both in absolute terms and in relation to sugar. Our interpretation is based on the Index of Agriculture Production (1972 = 100) derived by the Central Bank of Barbados for the period 1969–77. The Index of Agriculture Production shows a sharp decline of export agriculture from 118.4 in 1969 to 97.3 in 1977. Of course, the major cause was the secular decline of the sugar industry, which carries the highest weight in the index. Overall domestic food crop production also declined sharply during the period 1970–77. Especially sharp were reductions in the production of root crops such as yams and sweet potatoes, which carry the highest weights in the category.[11] The Index of Agriculture has not been published since 1977.

The only category to show an increase in output during the period 1970–77 was livestock products, especially the production of poultry products and milk. During the 1980s the performance of non-sugar agriculture fluctuated from year to year without any clear trend. However, the contribution of non-sugar agriculture during the 1990s was higher than sugar. By 2000 the contribution of non-sugar agriculture to the GDP was 3.0 percent compared with 1.5 percent for sugar.

Another area worthy of note is the fishing industry. As early as 1946, the fishing industry benefited from important institution supports, such as credit facilities.[12] After 1954, efforts were made to mechanize the fishing industry with financial assistance from the government, and complete mechanization was achieved in 1961. The industry also expanded with the growth of the export-oriented shrimp industry after 1963.[13] However, in 1978 the government took the decision to phase out the operation of its wholly owned company, International Seafoods Limited. Shrimping had become nonviable, partly because of the high maintenance costs of the fishing vessels (Barbados Government 1979–83:86. Between 1978 and 2000, government made no significant attempts to revive the shrimp industry.

CRITICAL APPRAISAL

A large part of the blame for the deterioration of post-war agriculture must be apportioned to the policy-makers. There were fundamental deficiencies in policy towards the estate sector and the small farmer. In the first place the heavy subdivision of agricultural land in the late 1960s into two- and four-acre lots led to further fragmentation of the agricultural sector and underutilization of land. This political factor initiated the decline of the sugar industry. The social cost of the subdivisions far outweighed the political and economic benefits accruing to those individuals who invested largely for real estate purposes. The attempt by government in the late 1970s to get agriculture land back into production was highly commendable and helped to halt the decline in agricultural output. However, in the 1980s the immediate objectives of agriculture policy were to halt further alienation of arable land to non-agricultural development and restore idle land to productive uses. Trade liberalization created a new issue in the 1990s, and its impact on the agricultural sector will be analysed in Chapter 10.

There was no well articulated policy towards the small farmer in the 1960s and early 1970s. Small farmers continued to suffer adversely from poor quality land, lack of capital, food crop losses from praedial larceny and poor marketing outlets. No serious efforts were made to organize farmers into cooperatives to increase economies of scale in food crop production. The continued fragmentation of peasant lands reduced technical efficiency in farm management because most of these fragmented units were cultivated in sugar, which is more suited to intermediate-scale farming. The small farmer was not convinced of the need to diversify away from sugar because he was given no guarantee that the costs and risks associated with food crop production would be alleviated.

The fundamental problem of devising a policy for the small farm sector also stems from the lack of information on the operations of small farms. Small farmers seldom keep accounts on the purchase or sale of their produce. As a result, it is difficult to estimate the productivity, profitability or the use to which capital is put in the small farm sector. This lack of accounting information often makes it difficult for small farmers to obtain credit. Government needs to decide whether the small farmer is to play a vibrant role in Barbadian agriculture.

Poor marketing outlets for his produce aggravate the problems of the small farmer. The Barbados Marketing Corporation was unable to deal adequately with shortages and surpluses of food crops. In the past this corporation lacked adequate storage and processing facilities and many buyers complained of the inferior quality commodities offered by the corporation. As a result of the inefficiencies of this institution, many small farmers had to face the uncertainties of disposing of their produce in the open market.

Mechanization was a positive step towards rationalization of the sugar industry, although small peasant farms did not justify the use of large machines. The introduction of green cane harvesters reduced many of the hazards associated with the burning of canes, particularly the sharp decline in cane yields. The mechanical loading of canes has also reduced some of the time spent in getting canes to the factories.

A study by the Barbados Ministry of Agriculture (2002c) helps us to identify certain strengths, weaknesses, opportunities and threats (SWOT) related to the agricultural sector by the year 2000. Such SWOT analysis is important in deciding a strategic plan for the sector. Among the strengths of the sector are the strong demand for local fresh produce, farmers' knowledge of production techniques, a well developed transport network to major markets, the presence of internationally renowned products such as sea island cotton, Barbados Black Belly sheep and Barbados cherry. The sector also has a competitive advantage in commodities such as yam, hot pepper and sweet potato, as well as a vibrant fisheries sector.

Despite the above strengths, however, agricultural development can be viewed with a certain degree of pessimism because the plantation system continues to be a burden on the society. This system's demand for finance is disproportionately high in relation to its output. The problem is that estate cultivation has long ceased to be economical, and government's previous land reform policies have worsened rather than alleviated the conditions of export agriculture.

The other major weaknesses already identified are high production costs, low productivity, lack of accurate and reliable information, weak farmers' organizations, seasonality of production, leading to fluctuations in prices and farmers' income, underdeveloped marketing systems, and small farm size. The few opportunities noted by the Barbados Agricultural

Planning Unit include strong niche market potential for sea island cotton, Barbados Black Belly sheep and Barbados cherry. Liberalization can increase exports but it also increases imports, leading to one of the major threats, namely cheap, subsidized imports (see Barbados Ministry of Agriculture 2002c:16, 17).

6

The Industrialization Process

INTRODUCTION

This chapter makes no attempt to survey all aspects of the manufacturing industry in Barbados. Rather, it focuses on the extent of domestic and foreign investment in manufacturing, labour and capital intensity, the degree of import substitution, and capacity utilization in manufacturing. Export promotion of manufactured goods is a theme of Chapter 9, and manufacturing finance is looked at in Chapter 10. Primarily as a result of limited availability of data for the 1960s, our analysis concentrates on the post-1970 industrialization process.[1]

MANUFACTURING UNDER COLONIAL DEVELOPMENT

Prior to 1960 the manufacturing sector was small and embryonic. In the early 1950s a few factories were engaged in the production of cigarettes, bay rum, nonalcoholic beverages and biscuits. There were also some small cottage industries as well as the potteries. Service-type, small-scale businesses usually comprised dressmaking and tailoring. The Colonial Office estimated that in 1946, of the 18,803 people involved in sugar factory operations and manufacturing, 7,563 were own-account workers in artisan-type activities, namely dressmaking and tailoring (Colonial Office 1953b). However, there is very little direct statistical information on the value of nonsugar manufacturing before 1957. GDP estimates of the value of manufacturing were derived largely from trade data and may have overstated actual values. The manufacturing surveys of 1957 and 1958 were the first to provide statistics on output and employment in manufacturing.[2] The 1958 survey showed that 3,195 people or 3.4 percent of the total labour force were employed in manufacturing. Of this number, 1,095 or 34 percent were employed in food and beverages. The food and beverage sectors contributed $9.5 million to the gross output of $17.7 million.

Table 6.1
Employment in Manufacturing (Selected Years)

Industry	1970	1975	1977	1980	1983	1985	1994
Food	1,191	1,306	1,498	1,220	1,650	1,655	1,884
Beverages	711	744	825	692	737	804	708
Wearing apparel	1,774	2,936	3,171	1,694	3,314	1,801	969
Furniture and fixtures	385	321	470	232	368	426	382
Printing and publishing	462	515	547	496	706	744	921
Chemicals	191	409	460	485	719	591	559
Nonmetallic mineral products	415	283	468	451	297	336	344
Fabricated metal products	283	449	462	462	991	645	707
Machinery and equipment	806	1,001	1,140	1,538	2,618	1,576	1,248
Other manufacturing	849	303	329	441	52	147	288
Total	7,067	8,267	9,370	7,711	11,452	8,725	8,010

Sources: Barbados Statistical Service, *Surveys of Industrial Establishments* (1970–85); *Industrial Census* (1994).

THE STRUCTURE OF MANUFACTURING AFTER 1970

An examination of the manufacturing sector with respect to its contribution to employment shows that wearing apparel operations employed the largest number of people up to 1985. This industry was followed by food manufacturing in the 1970s and machinery and equipment in the 1980s (see Table 6.1). The contribution to employment of wearing apparel fell from around 33.8 percent in 1977 to 20.6 percent in 1985. By 1994, the wearing apparel sector had declined significantly and food manufacturing became the major contributor to employment. By 2000 the manufacturing sector employed 10,400 workers or 8.0 percent of the employed labour force. This compares with other services (57.1 percent), commerce (14.8 percent) and construction (10.9 percent). The decline in external demand played an important role in restricting the growth of employment in manufacturing.

The analysis in Table 6.2 shows relatively high capital costs per job for 1976, 1977 and 1983. Comparable data were not available for the years after 1983. Jefferson (1971) and Cox (1987) have discussed the issue of high cost per job for Jamaica and Barbados, respectively. Cox estimates that the average cost per job for the period 1971–77 was $33,000. Jefferson interprets cost per job as an indication of high capital intensity. My interpretation of the analysis is that the initial cost per job concept is not a true capital/labour ratio. Capital expenditure is a flow concept, which varies from year to year, and gives no indication of the size or heterogeneity of the capital stock, either by sector or subsector. One should exercise

Table 6.2
Initial Capital Invested per Job in Manufacturing

	1970	1971	1972	1976	1977	1978	1983
New industries[a]	11	10	7	10	8	12	18
New jobs	460	383	362	443	232	307	334
Initial capital ($m) investment	0.9	2.9	1.4	9.7	15.1	3.1	12.4
Capital per job ($thousand)	1.9	7.6	3.9	21.9	65.1	10.1	37.1

[a] Refers to IDC-assisted industries starting operations.

Sources: Barbados Government, *Economic Surveys* (1970–80); Barbados Industrial Development Corporation, *Annual Reports* (1983–84).

Table 6.3
Percent Distribution of Value Added in Manufacturing (Selected Years)

Industry	1970	1975	1977	1980	1983	1985	1994
Food	20.7	12.5	14.1	20.2	13.4	25.3	17.9
Beverages	17.7	21.8	16.9	12.3	9.0	13.8	19.3
Wearing apparel	12.7	14.8	23.3	11.5	11.1	7.9	2.8
Furniture and fixtures	4.4	2.9	4.0	2.2	1.8	1.8	1.6
Printing and publishing	10.0	7.3	8.1	7.1	6.8	9.2	9.3
Chemicals	3.3	9.0	8.8	15.9	9.7	7.5	28.6
Nonmetallic mineral products	6.6	2.7	4.4	5.9	2.2	4.2	3.4
Fabricated metal products	3.7	13.8	5.4	6.5	13.2	5.4	6.7
Machinery and equipment	7.9	12.0	10.7	13.9	32.0	22.3	7.8
Other manufacturing	13.0	2.2	4.3	4.5	0.2	2.4	2.6
Total	100.0	100.0	100.0	100.0	100.0	100.0	100.0

Sources: Barbados Statistical Service, *Surveys of Industrial Establishments* (1970–85); *Industrial Census* (1994).

extreme caution in interpreting the initial cost per job concept as an operational measure of capital intensity. We return to this issue later.

Table 6.3 reports the contribution of each subsector to value added. Between 1970 and 1975, food, beverages and tobacco together were the major contributors. In the 1980s, though these sectors continued to contribute significantly, the machinery and equipment sector, which comprises electronic components, was the main contributor in 1983 and 1985. By 1994, chemicals, beverages and food were the main contributors.

The most important point for analysis, however, is that the rate of growth of employment fell behind the rate of growth of value added.

Between 1970 and 1994, the annual rate of growth of employment was 2.4 percent, while value added grew at a rate of 16 percent per annum. Baer and Herve (1966) have documented this tendency in developing countries. These authors sought to explain the phenomenon by reference to increased levels of labour productivity, high capital intensity, or both. In Barbados, gross output per head rose by 27.4 percent per annum between 1970 and 1994, indicating high levels of labour productivity. The existence of these factors in the Barbadian case may have been significant in explaining the low labour absorption rate in the manufacturing industry. We return to this point when we consider capital and labour intensities.

CAPITAL AND LABOUR INTENSITY

A well-known argument in the literature on industrialization in the Caribbean and other developing countries is that liberal tax incentives to foreign investors cheapen the cost of capital, thereby leading to high levels of capital intensity in the manufacturing industry. This argument, supported by some Caribbean economists in the 1960s, has not been tested extensively in the Caribbean context. A number of measures have been used to estimate capital and labour intensities in industry. Our discussion of these measures is based on an examination of the theses of Lary (1968) and Bhalla (1985). I examine theoretically the usefulness of four such measures: value added per employee (V/L); the share of wages in value added (W/V); the capital coefficient (K/V) and the capital labour ratio (K/L). My empirical analysis attempts to determine the usefulness of the V/L and W/V ratios in the measurement of labour intensity in Barbados.

Lary (1968) has employed the V/L ratio as an index of labour intensity. His argument is that the higher the V/L ratio the more capital intensive the industry; the lower the ratio the greater the degree of labour intensity. Lary's contention is that the use of this measure bypasses the difficulty of measuring physical capital. Bhalla (1985) has outlined the limitation of the usefulness of V/L as an index. The argument is that product market imperfections, such as monopoly, and high pricing policies of various firms will give rise to V/L differentials not attributable to differences in technical requirements of factor inputs. Technological differences, as well as inventory changes, depreciation charges and profit rates will also cause distortions in the V/L ratio. Differences in the nature of employment between firms (part-time or seasonal employment, etc.) will distort the comparability of V/L ratios.

Labour market imperfections also affect the W/V ratio, a measure used by Diaz-Alejandro (1965). Trade union aggressiveness and wage legislation distort factor prices and the share of wages in value added. In industries dominated by foreign enterprises, a high wages bill for expatriate executives may also give an upward bias to the W/V ratio. It does not always follow that a high W/V ratio is a good guide to the degree of labour intensity.

According to Bhalla (1985), the K/V ratio raises problems of measuring the capital stock. Nontechnological factors will also influence the denominator and numerator. The K/L ratio suffered from similar limitations such as interindustry differences in capital utilization and the heterogeneity of capital and labour. The K/L ratio is also limited by the bias of technical change and relative factor prices. The difficulty of finding data on the capital stock by industrial subsector precluded the use of this measure for Barbados.

We also noted Baer and Herve's (1966) use of installed power capacity per capita electricity consumption by industry groups as indicators of capital intensity. Their two measures equate capital intensity with energy utilization. One drawback is that certain types of capital equipment might be more energy efficient while having higher nominal costs. However, we were unable to obtain these data either by sector or subsector.

Nonetheless, bearing the above limitations in mind, I examined average W/V and V/L ratios for sample periods 1970–85 and 1980–85 (Table 6.4), as well as the *Industrial Census* (Barbados Statistical Service, 1994). The data on wages included wages paid to production workers as well as to workers not directly involved in production. It would have been preferable to use only wages paid to production workers, but I was unable to obtain such data.

Table 6.4
Measures of Labour Intensity (Annual Averages)

Industry	W/V (%) (1970–85)	Rank	V/L ($) (1970–85)	Rank	V/L ($) (1980–85)	Rank
Food	65.6	(4)	11,293	(7)	23,893	(8)
Beverages and tobacco	46.6	(9)	17,577	(9)	30,463	(9)
Wearing apparel	79.1	(2)	4,656	(1)	8,693	(2)
Furniture and fixtures	83.1	(1)	6,423	(2)	7,193	(1)
Printing and publishing	61.5	(5)	11,937	(8)	22,473	(6)
Chemicals	45.8	(10)	18,207	(10)	36,759	(10)
Nonmetallic mineral products	69.3	(3)	10,060	(4)	21,524	(5)
Fabricated metal products	56.9	(6)	10,138	(5)	17,086	(4)
Machinery and equipment	51.5	(8)	10,718	(6)	23,659	(7)
Other manufacturing	52.4	(7)	7,510	–	11,096	–
Sector average	57.2	–	10,255	–	20,990	–

Sources: Barbados Statistical Service, *Surveys of Industrial Establishments* (1970–85); *Industrial Census* (1994).

The W/V ratio shows that chemicals and beverages can be ranked highest in terms of capital intensity. Using the index, we find that at the other end of the spectrum furniture and wearing apparel can be ranked first and second, respectively, in terms of labour intensity. The fabricated metal products and machinery and equipment subsectors fall within an intermediate range below the industry average and all we can say is that these industries are less labour intensive (or more capital intensive) than clothing, wood and food products.

The V/L ratio for the period 1970–85 showed the same results for chemicals and beverages and a slightly different result for wearing apparel and furniture. Wearing apparel is ranked first as the most labour intensive industry when the V/L ratio is used. Other manufacturing is ranked third. The problem of classification again concerns the nonmetallic minerals, fabricated metals, and machinery and equipment subsectors, which fall within the intermediate range. Following Lary (1968) we can regard these industries as "marginally labour intensive", as their V/L ratios are near the overall sector average. The rankings for food, printing and publishing fall considerably when the V/L ratio is used.

Given the sharp rise of 37.1 percent in labour productivity between 1980 and 1985, we looked at the V/L ratio during this period to see if productivity growth was merely a result of higher levels of capital intensity. The analysis shows a few shifts in the rankings, with food and machinery and equipment ranking higher in terms of capital intensity. These industries showed sharp increases in value added. We can argue, however, that the 15.3 percent growth in value added and the annual fall of 1.7 percent in employment imply that there was an overall increase in capital intensity in the manufacturing sector as a whole between 1980 and 1985. Our result for this period confirms an earlier period trend observed by Downes (1985).

The *Industrial Census* (Barbados Statistical Service, 1994) confirmed the findings for labour and capital intensity for earlier periods. In 1994, the V/L ratio showed that chemicals, food manufacturing and machinery ranked highest in terms of capital intensity. Clothing and furniture had the highest levels of labour intensity.

LOCAL AND FOREIGN CAPITAL

Foreign capital was a significant proportion of initial capital invested in manufacturing in some years during the 1970s (Table 6.5). Much of this investment went to "off-shore" industries, such as electronics and plastics. Balance-of-payments data reported by Codrington (1987) show that between 1977 and 1980 foreign investment in the electronics components subsector was about 57.5 percent of foreign capital in manufacturing. This was followed by the chemical industry (21.7 percent). The data imply that,

Table 6.5
Distribution of Initial Foreign and Local Investment (1971–83)

Year	Initial Capital Investment ($m)	Foreign Capital ($m)	Local Capital ($m)	Foreign as a Percent of Total
1971	3.3	1.76	1.54	53.4
1972	2.8	2.38	0.42	85.1
1975	1.8	0.59	1.21	33.3
1977	8.2	7.49	0.71	91.4
1978	2.4	1.39	1.01	58.3
1980	11.2	4.50	6.70	40.0
1981	1.4	0.50	0.90	34.0
1982	5.7	0.84	3.76	14.7
1983	12.4	4.79	2.52	38.6

Note: Joint venture investment for 1982 and 1983 was $1.1 million and $5.1 million, respectively.

Source: Barbados Industrial Development Corporation, Annual Reports (1970–83).

given the high concentration of foreign capital in these two sectors, local capital was highly significant in other sectors, especially those catering for the domestic market.

Table 6.5 also reveals that local investment was more important in nominal magnitudes during the 1980s. Local investment in the Industrial Development Corporation (IDC)-assisted industries registered over 60 percent as a proportion of initial capital invested in manufacturing. There was also evidence of joint venture participation in the early 1980s. Local capital in the 1980s was not concentrated in any one subsector. The principal areas of investment were wearing apparel and fabrics, foods, chemicals, plastics and fabricated metal products. Between 1980 and 1985 local capital formation was high (over 90 percent of total capital formation) in the food sector.

Codrington's (1987) balance-of-payments data also support the observation relating to the decline in foreign capital in manufacturing. In 1977, foreign investment in manufacturing was $4 million or 24.2 percent of total foreign investment in the economy. By 1985, $3.2 million or 4.9 percent of total foreign investment was in manufacturing. The fall was due to recessionary conditions in the world economy between 1980 and 1984. These conditions significantly affected foreign investment in electronics and equipment.

Table 6.6 shows the distribution of foreign capital in manufacturing by subsector in the 1990s. The food and beverage subsector recorded the highest levels for the period. Table 6.7 reveals that Barbadians own most firms in the manufacturing sector, but this says nothing about the size of the firms.

Table 6.6
Foreign Investment in Manufacturing by Subsector (Bds $m)

Industry	1990	1991	1992	1993	1994
Food and beverages	10.40	8.13	12.30	10.21	0.80
Textiles	0.00	0.00	0.00	0.00	0.00
Chemicals	0.19	4.20	3.81	2.92	0.00
Wood furniture	0.00	0.00	6.21	0.00	0.00
Nonmetallic products	0.00	0.00	0.00	0.00	0.00
Basic metal products	0.66	1.37	1.48	0.00	0.00
Miscellaneous	0.61	0.71	0.00	1.00	0.00
Total	11.86	14.41	23.80	14.13	0.80

Source: A. Belgrave and W. Ward, *Foreign Direct Investment and the Barbadian Economy*, Working Papers, no. 2. (Bridgetown: Central Bank of Barbados, 1977), 88.

Table 6.7
Number of Firms in Manufacturing Classified by Ownership Status 1994

Ownership Status	Number	% of Total Ownership
100% owned by Barbadian nationals	189	70.3
50%–99% owned by Barbadian nationals	22	8.2
Over 50% owned by CARICOM nationals	9	3.3
Over 50% owned by other nationals	32	11.9
Not stated	17	6.3
Total	269	100.0

Source: Barbados Statistical Service, *Industrial Census* (1994).

Finally, our principal argument is that Barbadian policy-makers have to concentrate on raising the level of the country's international competitiveness to enhance manufacturing output. The contemporary period is characterized by trade liberalization and cross-border alliances between firms, which mean that Barbadian firms have to reposition themselves to take advantage of regional and international market opportunities. Barbados is a relatively high wage-cost producer, a factor reducing its international competitiveness. The high degree of worldwide competition in electronics and garments has also curtailed the flow of foreign investment to Barbados.

IMPORT SUBSTITUTION

Our third area of investigation is the measurement of the degree of import substitution, an operational feature of the Puerto Rican model, made possible by high levels of effective protection. In order to gauge the degree of reliance

Table 6.8
Domestic Sales as a Percentage of Total Sales (Selected Years)

Industry	1975	1980	1985	1994
Food	86	73	95	90
Beverages and tobacco	82	90	90	80
Wearing apparel	32	22	41	57
Furniture and fixtures	93	94	93	94
Printing and publishing	90	96	94	83
Chemicals	86	86	89	86
Nonmetallic mineral products	95	98	95	99
Other metal products	96	58	81	80
Machinery and equipment	42	26	22	20
Other manufacturing	5	3	80	80
All manufacturing	75	74	81	81

Sources: Barbados Statistical Service, *Surveys of Industrial Establishments* (1975, 1980, 1985); *Industrial Census* (1994).

on the domestic market in the Barbadian case, I examined samples of data between 1975 and 1994 on the market destination of industrial output.

Table 6.8 shows that generally, domestic sales comprise a very high proportion of total sales for most manufacturing subsectors between 1975 and 1985. The subsectors with the heaviest reliance on the domestic market are food, beverages and tobacco, furniture and fixtures, printing and publishing, chemicals and nonmetallic mineral products. The ratio of domestic sales to total sales for these sectors is over 90 percent in some years. The data also show the export orientation of the wearing apparel industry as well as industries producing machinery and equipment. Close analysis also reveals that the domestic market orientation for all industries remained high between 1985 and 1994. As the demand for exports declined, firms concentrated their efforts on the domestic market. This is examined later in the chapter on exports.

However, the division of manufacturing sales between the domestic and export markets is not enough evidence to inform us about the degree of import substitution. We need to examine the behaviour of the import coefficient and/or the output coefficient. The import coefficient is defined as the ratio of imports of a particular manufacturing category to total supplies, while the output coefficient is the ratio of domestic output to total supplies. Following Desai (1969) and Bhagwati and Desai (1970) I employed the following measures of import substitution.

Measure 1 — Import substitution is said to be positive if:

$$M2/S2 - M1/S1 < 0$$

Where
M = imports of competing goods
Q = domestic production
S = $Q + M$ = total supplies.

$M1$ and $S1$ are imports and total supplies, respectively, in the first period, and $M2$ and $S2$ are imports and total supplies in the second period.

Measure 2 — In this measure, the magnitude of import substitution is expressed as a proportion, that is, there is import substitution if:

$$(M2/S2 - M1/S1) / M1/S1 < 0$$

Measure 3 — This measure is given by:

$$[(Q2/S2 - Q1/S1) \, S2] / \Delta Q > 0$$

The change in the output coefficients must be positive for import substitution to take place.

The problem in applying these measures to the industry and trade data was the identification of competing imports. This was done by careful inspection of the computer printouts of Standard Industrial Trade Classification (SITC) trade data and comparing these data with the relevant International Standard Industrial Classification (ISIC) category. My estimates therefore contain some degree of error. I used two representative samples of data, 1971–75 and 1975–85. The results are reported in Tables 6.9 and 6.10. Table 6.9 gives the analysis for 1971–75 using five manufacturing categories: clothing, beverages and tobacco, furniture and fixtures, chemicals and machinery and equipment. These categories are clearly identifiable in the basket of imported goods. The category "food" is too heterogeneous to allow meaningful estimates to be made.

Table 6.9
Import Substitution (1971–75)

Industry	Measure 1	Measure 2	Measure 3
Clothing	0.08	34.0	−37.6
Beverages and tobacco	0.02	10.0	−5.6
Furniture and fixtures	−0.24	−54.0	94.0
Chemicals	−0.41	−51.0	72.3
Machinery and equipment	−0.02	−2.2	3.0

Source: Barbados Statistical Service, *Surveys of Industrial Establishments* (1971–75).

Table 6.10
Import Substitution (1975–85)

Industry	Measure 1	Measure 2	Measure 3
Clothing	–0.008	–2.5	1.9
Beverages and tobacco	–0.009	–4.0	1.9
Furniture and fixtures	–0.01	–5.0	2.0
Paper and paper products	–0.15	–30.0	29.5
Chemicals	–0.06	–16.0	13.2
Machinery and equipment	–0.133	–15.0	57.4

Source: Barbados Statistical Service, *Surveys of Industrial Establishments* (1975, 1985).

There was substantial import substitution in the categories furniture and fixtures and chemicals using all three measures. In the categories clothing, beverages and tobacco, there was no import substitution, because the import coefficient increased during the period. Measure three also shows that the output coefficient for clothing fell by 37.6 percent. The result for clothing is explained by the rise in competing imports from CARICOM and extraregional markets. The import coefficient fell slightly for machinery and equipment (see Table 6.9).

The analysis for the period 1975–85 in Table 6.10 shows that there was import substitution in all categories. Here we used six categories, including paper and paper products. For clothing and beverages and tobacco the fall in the import coefficient was very small, implying a very limited degree of import substitution. The degree of import substitution in furniture and chemicals is substantially less than in the previous period. The assembly of minibus bodies for the domestic market is the cause of the increase in import substitution in the category machinery and equipment. Overall, our analysis shows that import substitution has varied between industries. Import substitution is low for clothing and beverages, positive but declining for chemicals and furniture and reasonably high for transport equipment in the last period.

CAPACITY UTILIZATION IN MANUFACTURING

An early study by Little, Scitovsky and Scott (1970) found that developing countries recorded low capacity utilization in manufacturing. The authors attributed this to a number of reasons, among them the reluctance to operate more than a single shift and the insufficiency of imported materials. We examined the data for 1994 in Barbados provided by the Barbados Statistical Service's *Industrial Census 1994* (Table 6.11). The analysis showed that of the 225 firms surveyed, 116 (51 percent) had capacity utilization above 75 percent; 65 recorded capacity

Table 6.11
Capacity Utilization in Manufacturing by Subsector 1994

Industry	No. of Firms	Capital Utilization		
		Under 50%	50%–74%	75% and over
Food	41	10	11	20
Beverages and tobacco	12	4	4	4
Wearing apparel	43	10	17	16
Furniture and fixtures	32	7	8	17
Printing and publishing	24	2	7	15
Chemicals	17	5	4	8
Nonmetallic mineral products	6	1	1	4
Fabricated metal products	15	3	4	4
Machinery and equipment	15	1	1	13
Other manufacturing	20	1	8	11
Total	225	44	65	112

Source: Barbados Statistical Service, *Industrial Census* (1994).

utilization between 50 percent and 74 percent; while 10 were below 50 percent capacity. The highest levels of capacity utilization were registered by the machinery and equipment subsector, followed by nonmetallic mineral products and printing and publishing. Demand factors most likely explain why half of the number of firms had capacity utilization above 75 percent. The small domestic market reduces economies of scale. Further manufacturing in Barbados has been adversely affected by market liberalization, which forced firms to compete with imported substitutes.

SMALL BUSINESS MANUFACTURING

Our analysis of the small-business manufacturing sector is based on a survey by Lashley (2002). He analysed 146 manufacturing establishments between October and December 2001. Of these firms, 42 were micro-enterprises (i.e., employing five or fewer persons), 58 were small businesses (employing six to twenty-five persons), and 40 were medium or large (more than twenty-five persons). Lashley (2002) found the following characteristics:

1. Much of the competition was from local enterprises (55.2 percent), while only 6.9 percent was regional.
2. Most enterprises were locally oriented. The main customer base was considered local by 73.3 percent of respondents.
3. Most enterprises experiencing heavy local competition are not establishing any linkages with other firms to ameliorate this

problem. Non-cooperation may not allow these businesses to survive in the context of globalization.

4. Of the firms surveyed, 49.7 percent exported some of their output. The destination of exports was CARICOM (66.2 percent of respondents) followed by the United States (14.1 percent).

5. Most enterprises (34.3 percent) cited transport and freight charges as the most serious cost problem in exporting.

6. The most significant problems experienced by small enterprises were the cost of inputs, late payment for sales and operating costs.

Institutional support for small business is perhaps stronger than it was in the pre-1980 era. The Barbados Institute of Management and Productivity (BIMAP) and the Small Business Association have survived from the 1970s. The Central Bank and the Barbados National Bank (BNB) have set up schemes to finance small businesses. Two venture capital companies were also established in the 1990s. (See the section on financial innovation in Chapter 10.) The main financing needs of small businesses are working capital and access to long-term finance. Many small businesses, however, do not have the collateral to qualify for loans. This is where venture capital is important. Government continues to provide tax incentives and technical assistance to these businesses. Whitehall and Moore (2000) discuss these issues, as well as identify other agencies providing small business finance.

SUMMARY

The Barbadian manufacturing sector showed a low level of labour absorption. This is attributable to rising labour productivity, reduced external demand and high levels of capital intensity in a few industries, particularly food manufacturing and chemicals. The analysis indicated high levels of capital intensity in the period 1980–85. Although the wearing apparel industry is relatively labour-intensive, labour absorption levels in this industry have been significantly affected by the fall in external demand. Since it is difficult to substitute labour for capital in capital-using industries, the only policy option remaining is to increase exports in those sectors that are now presently geared for the domestic market.

The manufacturing industry in Barbados displayed an unreasonably high level of dependence on the domestic market. Home-based expansion has become even more important with the shrinkage of export markets in the 1980s and 1990s. Too heavy a dependence on the small domestic market limits employment expansion.

My analysis suggests that the role of the manufacturing sector in the Barbadian economy has been constrained by the difficulty of penetrating external markets and high wage costs. The result has been a heavy dependence on the domestic market and low levels of labour absorption. However, in the twenty-first century more attention will have to be focused on the promotion of skill-intensive industries, such as data processing, in order to meet the demands of the information age. Further, manufacturing must provide goods for the tourist sector, which became the leading foreign exchange earner after 1980. There is considerable scope for marketing food products, beverages, clothing and handicraft in the tourism industry.

Another important issue is that of low levels of international competitiveness in Barbadian manufacturing. Wage increases should not be so high as to hinder the absorption of the labour surplus and also reduce the competitiveness of industrial exports. Already it seems that high wage levels have reduced Barbados's international competitiveness.

7

Tourism and Offshore Business

INTRODUCTION

By 2000, the Barbadian economy had become almost completely dependent on tourism and other services for its survival. This chapter discusses a few pertinent issues relating to the growth of tourism and offshore business. Our analysis is concerned with tourism dependence, the ownership structure of the tourism plant, cost problems in the tourist sector during the 1980s and the impact of tourism on development. I also report the findings of Clarke, Wood and Worrell (1986) and Worrell, Greenidge, Downes and Dalrymple (1997) on the demand for tourism services in Barbados. This chapter also assesses the contribution of the offshore sector to employment, growth and government revenues.

THE NATURE OF TOURISM DEPENDENCE

Following Bryden (1975:91), two appropriate indicators of tourism dependence are the ratio of tourist receipts to GDP and the ratio of tourist receipts to exports of goods and services. Table 7.1 shows that the ratio of tourist receipts to GDP increased sharply between 1960 and 1970. Thereafter, the ratio declined slightly in the 1970s and stabilized at just over 28 percent in the 1980s. During the 1990s the ratio was well over 30 percent in most years. As a point of comparison, the Bahamas, which is a complete tourism economy, registered a ratio of tourist receipts to GDP of over 40 percent as early as the late 1970s. Tourist receipts as a ratio of exports of goods and services for Barbados are also quite high, reaching 82.9 percent in 2000, indicating Barbados's heavy dependence on this industry. The high ratio of tourist receipts to GDP and exports is also a measure of the gross contribution of tourism to foreign exchange earnings.

Tourism dependence is related to market expansion in the industrialized economies. The rapid growth of markets in the 1960s led to heavy investment in the tourism plant. Shankland Cox Partnership (1974) estimated that fifteen new hotels were built between 1965 and 1970. The hotel boom was propelled by foreign investment made possible under the Hotels Aids Act of 1967. Although it is difficult to estimate the volume of foreign investment attributable to this Act, Shankland Cox Partnership

Table 7.1
Indicators of Barbados's Tourism Dependence (Selected Years)

Year	Tourist Arrivals	Tourist Receipts (TR) (Bds. $million)	TR as % of Exports[a]	TR as % of GDP
1960	–	14.0	–	11.5
1964	–	24.0	–	16.2
1970	156,417.0	81.0	39.7	31.2
1974	230,718.0	157.0	51.1	27.1
1978	316,883.0	270.0	50.6	28.8
1982	303,995.0	502.0	51.3	28.2
1985	359,135.0	647.0	50.1	28.2
1992	385,472.0	925.0	77.5	34.2
1995	442,107.0	1,224.0	81.7	38.7
1998	512,397.0	1,406.0	81.6	35.9
1999	514,614.0	1,332.0	78.6	32.2
2000	544,696.0	1,422.0	82.9	33.1

[a] Denotes total exports of goods and services.

Sources: Central Bank of Barbados, *Annual Statistical Digest* (various years); Barbados Statistical Service, *Survey of Accommodation Establishments* (1984, 1985); Barbados Statistical Service, *Digest of Tourism Statistics* (2001).

(1974) has presented data to show that for the years 1968 to 1970, total investment in Barbados amounted to US $36.9 million. Further, foreigners controlled over 60 percent of hotel bed capacity between 1970 and 1971. The heavy foreign investment in tourism, which is also a measure of structural dependence, leads us to a consideration of the ownership of the tourism plant.

OWNERSHIP OF THE TOURISM PLANT

Early fiscal incentive legislation was designed to encourage foreign investment in tourism. The Barbados Hotels Aids Act 1967 was the counterpart of the Pioneering Industry's Act of 1958. The Hotels Aids Act guaranteed income and profits tax exemption for ten years and free entry of building materials. There was a bias in the legislation that encouraged the building of large hotels, thereby preventing many local Barbadians from hotel ownership. This policy was modified, however, in the Amendment to the Hotels Aids Act 1973, which stated that Barbadian nationals should be given concessions to build hotels with less than twenty-five rooms, and apartments with less than fifty units. Increased local ownership is desirable because it has implications for higher levels of local management and control of the industry.

Table 7.2
Ownership of Hotels in Barbados 1971

| Category of Accommodation | No. of Hotels | | Percent |
	Locally Owned	Foreign Owned	Locally Owned
Luxury hotels	3	10	23
Class "A" hotels	3	8	27
Class "B" hotels	6	5	55
Class "C" hotels	2	1	67
Apartment hotels	20	12	63
Guest houses	10	–	100
Total	44	36	55

Source: The Shankland Cox Partnership, *Tourism Supply in the Caribbean Region* (Washington, DC: World Bank, 1974), Table 1C.

The pattern of hotel ownership in the 1970s reflected the early bias in the incentive legislation. Table 7.2 shows the distribution of hotel ownership in Barbados in 1971. Foreign ownership was concentrated in large luxury hotels and "A" class hotels. Of the thirteen luxury hotels then in existence, only 23 percent were locally owned, while 27 percent of "A" class hotels were owned by Barbadians. The highest proportion of local ownership was concentrated in "C" class and apartment hotels and guesthouses. Shankland Cox's (1974) data do not provide a detailed description of the distribution of ownership according to bed capacity or the value of investment in hotels by ownership. Watson (1974), using alternative data for 1970–71, posited that 64 percent of hotel bed capacity was under foreign control. Locals controlled 91 percent and 92 percent of bed capacity in guest houses and apartments, respectively.

The *Ministry of Tourism Survey 1979*, carried out by the Ministry of Tourism, Barbados revealed that 74 percent of the bed capacity of luxury hotels in Barbados in 1978 was foreign owned, while class two and class three hotels were predominantly locally owned. Overall, foreign ownership comprised 55.7 percent of total hotel bed capacity. Local ownership was confined predominantly to guest houses, apartments and apartment hotels. Further, foreigners owned thirty-six establishments, and the proportion of their investment of $68.5 million was 48.2 percent. Locals owned eighty-four establishments and contributed $73.6 million or 51.8 percent to investment.

Further analysis for the 1980s shows that the pattern of hotel ownership established in the past has been modified to the extent that Barbadian ownership has increased in luxury class hotels. The data in Table 7.3 reveal this clearly. Foreigners other than CARICOM nationals owned 52.6 percent

Table 7.3
Ownership of Tourism Establishments 1985 (Percentages)

Category	No. of Rooms	Locally Owned	CARICOM Nationals	Other Foreign
Hotels	1,867	50.3	1.7	48.0
Group I	1,421	45.2	2.2	52.6
Group II	231	39.0	0.0	61.3
Group III	215	96.3	0.0	3.7
Apartment hotels	1,605	47.5	11.8	40.8
Group I	1,027	24.5	13.7	61.8
Group II	442	89.1	10.9	0.0
Group III	136	86.0	0.0	14.0
Apartments	1,256	86.3	8.2	5.6
Guest houses	76	100.0	0.0	0.0
Total	4,804	59.6	6.7	33.7

Source: Barbados Statistical Service, *Survey of Accommodation Establishments* (1984, 1985).

of group I hotels while Barbadians owned 45.2 percent. Foreign ownership was still strong in group I apartment hotels. Whereas in 1978 foreign ownership comprised 55.7 percent of total hotel bed capacity, by 1985 this had fallen to 40.4 percent.

Recent data provided by the Barbados Tourism Authority for the year 2000 showed that, of the seventy hotels, twenty-six were more than 75 percent Barbadian owned. Of the eighty-seven apartments and guest houses, thirty-eight were more than 75 percent Barbadian owned. However, these data are not detailed enough to make firm comparisons with past trends in foreign and local ownership.

REVIEW OF TOURISM'S IMPACT ON DEVELOPMENT

Previous research to measure the net macro impact of tourism on the Barbadian economy has taken the form of multiplier analysis and input-output analysis. Zinder and Associates (1969) carried out the multiplier analysis, while Armstrong, Daniel and Francis (1974) estimated input-output coefficients for Barbados. Bryden and Faber (1971) and Levitt and Gulati (1970) criticized Zinder and Associates' multiplier analysis for failing to come to grips with the orthodox theory of income multipliers. The approach of Armstrong et al. (1974) shed some light on the direction of tourism's impact on other sectors of the economy. Two other areas of interest are the "leakage" and employment effects of tourism analysed by Doxey and Associates (1971) and Marshall (1977), respectively. All of these efforts were highly tentative because they were not grounded on a clear definition of the tourism sector, and the underlying data base was fragmentary. However, they do warn us about the pitfalls of estimating tourism's net contribution in a highly open economy such as that of Barbados.

Zinder and Associates (1969) argued that the multiplier effect of one tourist dollar spent in the economy of Barbados was 2.3, before the impact wore off through leakages. The criticisms levelled at Zinder's approach illustrated the difficulties of applying multiplier-type analysis to the tourism industry. Bryden and Faber pointed out that Zinder merely added together a number of nominal income transactions without taking into consideration import leakages. Bryden and Faber (1971) carried out their own research to obtain an "income-to-nationals" (ITN) multiplier of between 0.8 and 0.9 for Antigua. They argued that the relevant multiplier is more likely to be less than one for the Eastern Caribbean and hardly as high as the 2.3 claimed for it by the Zinder Report.

The input-output analysis by Armstrong et al. was the first serious attempt to measure the relationship between tourism and the rest of the economy. The analysis revealed that the tourist dollar generated the highest proportion of output in hotels, other services, utilities, transport and communications, and other manufactures. Linkages with agriculture, distribution and construction were relatively low. They also estimated that one dollar's worth of tourist spending generated, directly and indirectly, one dollar and forty-one cents of output over all industrial sectors. Their analysis also led to the conclusion that the primary input content of the tourist dollar into imports was 33 percent. However, this estimate excluded profits accruing to foreigners operating in the economy as a whole. The import coefficient was measured in terms of raw materials of productive goods and services and therefore understates the leakage abroad. Doxey's (1971) alternative estimate of the leakage of tourist expenditure abroad was 42 percent.

Further investigations have shown that the impact of the tourism industry on public utilities, especially electricity, was quite high, particularly after the oil crisis of 1973–74. This also has implications for the leakage of the tourist dollar abroad to pay for imports of petroleum to generate electricity. Holder (1978) estimated that between 1972 and 1977 the tourism industry in Barbados consumed 15 percent to 16 percent of total electricity. Oil and gas rose 16.18 percent between 1973 and 1974, and 111.95 percent between 1973 and 1977. It is contended that the rapid increases in oil prices after 1973 not only pushed up the operating costs of the hotel industry, but may also have significantly accelerated the leakage of the tourist dollar abroad. Also, the sharp growth in nominal tourist receipts noted earlier is probably a reflection of rising costs in the hotel industry after 1973, stemming from higher oil prices.

Available evidence also suggests that during the early 1980s the high level of cost in the hotel industry was a severe constraint on the extent to which the industry could make further contribution to employment and

Table 7.4
Cost Indicators in Tourism Establishments (Percentages)

All Establishments	1971	1972	1984	1985
Labour cost/total income	23.7	22.8	34.1	32.2
Other costs/total income	62.8	61.7	78.3	75.0
Valued added/total income	42.7	43.7	28.4	31.7
Net profit (loss)/total income	13.4	15.5	(12.3)	(7.2)

Source: Barbados Statistical Service, *Survey of Accommodation Establishments* (1984, 1985).

growth. The recessionary conditions of 1981–85, high interest rates and wage costs imposed severe financial hardship on hotel operators. Wage rates, interest and maintenance costs constituted over 50 percent of operating costs in the 1980s. Table 7.4 provides indicators to show that the ratio of labour costs and other costs to operating income rose significantly after 1971. The analysis also reveals that the ratio of value added to income fell and that the industry experienced losses in 1984 and 1985, as shown by the ratio of net losses to total income. The government attempted to ease the financial stringency of the hotel industry in its 1986 budget by reducing hotel property tax rates by 50 percent. The reduction of costs was important to maintaining Barbados's price competitiveness as a tourist destination. Data were not available after 1985 to analyse costs in the Barbadian tourism industry.

The direct contribution of tourism to employment is not as high as in the manufacturing industry. However, its indirect contribution, which is more difficult to estimate, is highly significant. Marshall's (1977) work on Barbados during the 1970s is the only comprehensive study to analyse tourism's role as a generator of employment. Her study attempted to estimate the level of indirect employment in tourism as well as employee per room ratios in the hotel industry. However, estimates of direct employment were obtained from the Barbados Statistical Service, the *Barbados Development Plan* 1973–77 and the Central Bank of Barbados. These estimates, which are shown in Table 7.5, reveal that direct employment as a ratio of the labour force was relatively low up to 1985, falling from a high of 4.7 percent in 1975 to 3.7 percent in 1985 despite the expansion in the tourism plant.

By the year 2000, direct employment in tourism had risen to 10.1 percent of the labour force. I was unable to find a scientific estimate of indirect employment in tourism for the entire survey period. Marshall (1977) gives an estimate of 7,364 for 1975 or 7 percent of the labour force. The evidence also seems to indicate that the hotel sector was not very labour-intensive in the 1980s. This is shown by the low employee per

Table 7.5
Direct Employment in Tourism

Year	Employed ('000 Persons)	Tourism Employment as % of Labour Force
1970	4.1	4.4
1971	3.8	4.1
1975	4.9	4.7
1984	4.1	3.6
1985	4.2	3.7
1991	9.5	7.3
1992	9.8	7.4
1993	9.4	7.1
1994	11.1	8.2
1995	11.9	8.7
1996	12.3	9.1
1997	12.3	9.1
1998	14.0	10.1
1999	12.5	8.1
2000	14.5	10.1

Sources: Barbados Statistical Service, Barbados Development Plan (1973–77); Central Bank of Barbados, Annual Statistical Digest (2002).

room ratio of 0.9 in the 1980s. The low ratio is primarily explained by employee per room ratios lower than one in establishments other than luxury hotels and group I apartment hotels. Even so, the employee per room ratio of 1.2 recorded for luxury hotels in 1984 and 1985 is much lower than the 1.7 found by Shankland Cox Partnership (1974) for 1971, and Marshall's (1977) estimate of 2.01 in 1972. I was unable to find evidence on employee per room ratios for the 1990s.

Another issue of importance in the development of tourism is the role of international competitiveness. Worrell, Boamah and Campbell (1996) reported that during the 1980s and early 1990s the relative price of Barbados's tourism increased faster than its Caribbean competitors, implying that Barbados was less internationally competitive. Further, they argued that Barbados lost its market share continuously over the 1980s and 1990s within the Caribbean group comprising Puerto Rico, the Bahamas and Jamaica. This occurred even though Barbados's wages grew slower than prices. Wage moderation was also combined with increases in productivity in tourism. It appears that repeated devaluations by Barbados's competitors were the main source of their price advantage (Worrell, Boamah and Campbell 1996:20).

Finally, research on tourism in Barbados in the 1980s and 1990s focused on estimating tourism demand, rather than its macro impact on the economy. This orientation of research is appropriate because it has implications for revitalizing the tourism industry, since Barbados has become a mature tourist destination. Two studies by Clarke, Wood and Worrell (1986) and Worrell et al. (1997) estimated the demand for tourism services in Barbados. Clarke et al. found that per capita incomes in the source countries such as the United States, Canada and the United Kingdom were the most important explanatory factors. Worrell et al. (1997) reaffirmed the importance of the income variable, and also noted that unit labour cost in Barbados was the principal factor affecting the price of the tourism product.

OFFSHORE BUSINESS

Barbados has promoted offshore business in an attempt to accelerate economic development. An offshore centre facilitates financial transactions between nonresidents by means of low taxation and relief from exchange controls. The main characteristics of offshore centres are low licence fees and low or no relevant taxes on transactions. The institutions found in offshore centres such as Barbados are offshore banks, captive insurance companies, societies with restricted liability, international business companies, foreign sales corporations, ship registries, mutual funds, trusts and holding companies. They are established to conduct operations in the context of lower taxes, fees and licences than exist in their country of origin.

It is appropriate to outline the types of offshore business operating in Barbados. Our description borrows from Schoen (1996), Nicholls (1999), Evans (1999), DeCaires (1999) and Tibbitts (1999). The International Business Companies Act allows international business companies (IBCs) to engage in international manufacturing, international trade or commerce using Barbados as a domicile. IBCs pay annual licence fees and are taxed at rates ranging from 1 percent to 2.5 percent on their profits. IBCs are exempt from withholding tax on dividends, interest, fees and royalties. IBCs are also exempt from exchange controls and duties on imports.

Offshore banks (OBs) accept deposits from nonresidents and lend to other nonresidents in a currency other than that of the host country. They also accept foreign securities. Like IBCs, they pay annual licence fees and are taxed at the same tax rate on their profits. OBs are also exempt from withholding taxes and exchange controls but they are required to file financial statements with the Central Bank. The economic contribution of OBs is discussed later.

According to DeCaires (1999:36), a foreign sales corporation (FSC) "is a separate foreign corporation incorporated in an approved jurisdiction outside the United States that elects, with the consent of its shareholders, to be treated as an FSC". In 1984 the FSC was established by the United States Congress to provide an incentive for US companies to export products manufactured in the United States by providing an exemption from US tax on export profits. A US company can qualify for FSC benefits by establishing a corporation in a qualifying US possession or foreign country. The FSC must have its main office in Barbados or other qualifying destination. There must be a nonresident director and its accounts must be kept in Barbados. The FSC is also exempt from withholding taxes and exchange controls. The reader is referred to Schoen (1996) and DeCaires (1999) for further details on FSC operations.

An exempt or captive insurance company (CIC) insures the risks of its shareholders or parent company. In Barbados these companies are exempt from income taxation and withholding taxes. Some CICs are also involved in the international reinsurance market (see Evans 1999).

Societies with restricted liability (SRLs) in Barbados were created under the Society with Restricted Liabilities Act of 1995. The SRL is a corporate entity that has a full corporate personality and limited liability. An SRL can be an exempt society and can transact business in Barbados with other exempt societies, OBs, IBCs and CICs. An exempt society pays taxes ranging from 1.00 percent to 2.50 percent on its profits. An exempt SRL cannot acquire land in Barbados, other than land required for its business, held by way of lease or tenancy agreement. For a further discussion of the 1995 Act see Tibbitts (1999).

Our comments on the economic contribution of offshore business in Barbados will be brief because of the sparse data. Further, the operations of these companies have not been heavily researched. The discussion therefore leans on Doyle and Johnson (1999) in an attempt to identify the contribution of offshore companies to employment, output and government revenues.

Doyle and Johnson (1999) produced data to show that in 1998 the number of offshore companies in Barbados was 5,606 compared with 2,346 in 1993. Most of these companies were IBCs, which totalled 2,872 in 1998 or 51.2 percent of the total. These were followed by FSCs (42.6 percent). In 1998, there were two hundred exempt insurance companies, thirty-two exempt insurance management companies, sixty-five societies with restricted liability and forty-four offshore banks.

Doyle and Johnson (1999) estimate that the net foreign exchange earnings of all offshore companies averaged $110 million between 1995 and 1997, second only to tourism. Offshore companies are allowed to hold only foreign currency and are restricted from borrowing in the local financial market. Doyle and Johnson therefore suggest that funds spent by these businesses on government taxes, labour and goods or services are considered foreign exchange earnings for the economy. However, there is no way of testing the validity of these estimates, because it is not easy to estimate the leakage of foreign exchange. The analysis of Doyle and Johnson should therefore be regarded as highly tentative.

Employment in offshore centres tends to be low relative to the sales and profits generated. We were unable to find actual data on job creation in the offshore sector. Further, there is no firm data on the sector's contribution to GDP. Doyle and Johnson (1999:14) estimate that offshore banks contributed $1.77 billion to GDP or 35.2 percent of GDP from services. This exceeded tourism's contribution of 9.6 percent of service GDP. Again, given the difficulty of estimating service value added, their estimates must be interpreted with great caution. (See also the section on financial innovation in Chapter 10 for further information on OBs.)

SUMMARY

Barbados's dependence on tourism must be evaluated in the light of the decline in the sugar sector and the moderate performance of manufacturing. Tourism has an impact on the rest of the economy in terms of foreign exchange, employment in related services and its overall contribution to economic growth. Its impact on utilities should be regarded as a cost to the economy in terms of foreign exchange. The magnitude of the leakage of the tourist dollar abroad is difficult to measure in view of the diversity of tourist spending on imports as well as the export of profits and dividends not only from hotels but also from other establishments catering to tourists, such as duty free shops and multinational firms. Despite its net development impact, the tourism industry has been plagued with the problem of rising operating costs in tourism establishments. A principal objective of government policy was to reduce operating costs in order to increase the industry's competitiveness in the world market.

Our analysis of the offshore sector was highly tentative. Owing to the absence of firm data on the sector's contribution to GDP, foreign exchange and employment, we were unable to make definitive statements on the offshore sector's contribution to economic development.

8

Labour and Human Resource Development

INTRODUCTION

The structural processes we have described necessarily affected the distribution of labour resources in the economy. We need to examine the shift of labour from the primary to the service sectors of the economy. An important related question is the extent to which labour migrated to relieve structural pressures in the domestic economy. The above issues also raise questions about the magnitude of unemployment. Was unemployment substantially reduced during the process of dependence structural change and migration? Let us turn to an analysis of these issues.

THE FISHER/CLARKE THESIS

A line of inquiry associated with the original work of Fisher (1939) and Clarke (1957) is that economic progress leads to a shift of employment from primary towards secondary and tertiary activities. The original Fisher/Clarke thesis relates this tendency to market forces stemming from the relatively higher elasticities of demand for tertiary products. As a result, the demand for tertiary products increases more rapidly with economic progress. It is arguable that, although there was a definite shift of labour in the Barbadian economy to tertiary activity, this was primarily attributable to the structural processes described in previous chapters rather than to a law of market forces. I also agree with Bauer and Yamey (1965) that one must examine the nature of economic specialization rather than impose uncritically the Fisher/Clarke interpretation on occupation statistics in developing countries.

Lewis's observations (1955:340) on the shift of labour between sectors underline the complexities of the transition process in a manner not analysed by Fisher and Clarke. Lewis's remarks are relevant to labour reallocation processes in small, open economies. The transfer of labour from primary to tertiary activity can take place "without embarrassment" only if agricultural productivity is increasing, or if there is a rise in the export of non-agricultural commodities. That is, if there is no increase in agricultural productivity, labour must go to industries, which earn foreign exchange with which to purchase food, either by saving on imports, or by increasing exports. Lewis's analysis helps us to understand some aspects of the distribution of labour in Barbados after 1960.

However, before 1960 the principal means of relieving surplus labour on the land was state-aided migration, since there was no significant transfer of productive activity from the primary sector. The accelerated structural changes after 1960 led to the expansion of foreign exchange earners, such as tourism and exports of manufactures, which compensated for the decline in agricultural output, and enabled labour to shift from agriculture to other sectors without embarrassment. Thus, the government's policy of diversification also explains the perceived shift of labour after 1960.

THE MIGRATION RESPONSE

The migration response in the labour surplus economy of the 1950s was of course related to push factors operating in the domestic economy as well as pull factors in the metropolitan countries. This section focuses on the peak years of migration between 1946 and 1964. Two important theoretical approaches have been used to explain the push factors influencing early post-war migration. First, the Malthusian approach views migration as a temporary palliative to population pressure. This was the view held by most policy-makers in Barbados during the 1940s and 1950s. Barbados was regarded as a vastly overpopulated country, and unemployment was a result of overpopulation. State-aided emigration was a partial solution to these problems.[1]

The Marxist critique of Malthusian theory advances the view that demographic factors can only be explained in relation to the prevailing organization of social production. In Marxist theory, there is a tendency for the volume of wage labour purchased by variable capital to decline as capitalist accumulation proceeds. Migration is a means of reducing this domestic "reserved army" of the unemployed.[2]

Admittedly, a fundamental reason for migration stemmed from the structure of the early post-war Barbadian economy. The persistence of monoculture and technology improvements in the sugar industry led to a reduction in the demand for labour, in keeping with Marxist theory. This view is partial, however, because it does not explore the conditions of the metropolitan economies after the war. Migration was also a function of decisions made in the metropole relating to its "absorptive capacity" for foreign supplies of labour. This is illustrated when we examine below the impact of the Commonwealth Immigrants Act of 1962 and Canadian

Table 8.1
Emigration to the United Kingdom from Barbados (1957–66)

Year	Total	Sponsored Emigrants	Sponsored as % of Total
1957	1,851	650	35
1958	1,242	359	28.9
1959	1,154	464	40.2
1960	4,194	1,011	24.1
1961	6,013	978	16.6
1962	3,704	1,315	35.5
1963	1,849	1,499	81.9
1964	2,437	972	39.9
1965	NA	1,350	NA
1966	NA	420	NA

Note: NA = not available.

Source: Barbados, Ministry of Finance, *Economic Surveys* (1964–70).

immigration policy. Further, the United Kingdom had to resort initially to foreign labour to keep its public utilities going. This was particularly the case in the health services and transport. Additionally, other pull factors influencing migrants were higher wages and the prospects of better economic opportunities in the metropole. Thus, migration in the 1950s must be explained in terms of an interdependency relationship, especially in the case of the United Kingdom, which absorbed a large inflow of permanent migrants from the Caribbean.

The origins of post-war emigration are to be found partly in the exigencies of World War II. Barbadian workers were recruited on a contract basis to work in the United States as early as 1944.[3] Many Barbadians who were employed in the British armed forces returned to Britain after finding it difficult to obtain jobs at home. State-aided migration in Barbados immediately after World War II rested on three basic schemes: the sponsored permanent migration scheme; the loans guarantee scheme for either sponsored or unsponsored emigrants; and temporary contract migration. The sponsored permanent migration scheme to assist migration to Britain started in 1950. According to Davison (1962) the migrants to Britain went to a variety of occupations principally in transport, hotels and medical services.[4] Table 8.1 shows that the proportion of sponsored emigrants was generally lower than that of unsponsored emigrants. The proportions fluctuate markedly and it is difficult to determine a clear pattern. Emigrants could also qualify for an enabling loan from the Government of Barbados, provided they had a local guarantor and sufficient collateral. According to Davison most loans went to people travelling under the official recruitment scheme, as they were most likely to have a bona fide offer of employment abroad. Emigration to the United Kingdom continued in large numbers, rising rapidly to 6,013 in 1961. This large increase was most likely to evade the band foreseen on Commonwealth emigration to Britain. The Commonwealth Immigrants Act was introduced in 1962 to curb emigration to Britain by stating that Commonwealth emigrants should possess work permits when seeking entry to Britain. The full impact of the Act was not felt until 1966 when the number of sponsored workers was reduced from 1,315 in 1965 to 420 in 1966. The Commonwealth Immigrants Act showed to a large extent that migration from the colonies was intimately related to economic decisions made in Britain.

Contract emigration to the United States was another instrument of government policy to reduce unemployment and population pressure.[5] This category of emigration showed a high degree of annual variation. The peak period of emigration was between 1959 and 1964, when the number of emigrants averaged just over 1,000 per annum. In 1963, contract emigration to the United States reached a peak of 1,907 people. However, it is difficult to obtain data on the numbers of persons who emigrated permanently to the United States during the period 1964–2000. It is also problematic to ascertain the numbers who emigrated on a temporary basis and became permanent migrants. Palmer (1979) has reported that between 1962 and 1976 the number of Barbadians emigrating to the United States was 18,514. The landed immigrant status of these people was not given.

Early post-war emigration to Canada was small. This was primarily a result of Canada's restrictive immigration policy, according to Passaris (1979:297–300). Canada's immigration policy was based on a preoccupation with absorptive capacity, which depended on the level of economic activity and employment conditions in Canada. Canada's immigration policy since 1952 has stressed that immigrants should be selected on the basis of professional or technical skills, which effectively debarred many Barbadians from entry during the early post-war period. The Canadian regulations were designed to reduce competition between Canadians and immigrants for available jobs. Sponsored permanent emigration to Canada related solely to the domestic workers' scheme. The quota of emigrants under this scheme varied between twenty-five in 1955 and forty-three in 1960. The government also made loans to non-sponsored emigrants who could produce evidence of guaranteed employment. The numbers of such emigrants were also small (averaging under 200 per year) and comprised mainly students. There are no reliable statistics on unsponsored emigration to Canada after 1964. During the 1970s, the Government of Barbados encouraged contract migration to Canada. The peak period of migration under the farm labour contract scheme was 1976–80 when the number of migrants exceeded 1,300 (see Table 8.4).

Table 8.2
Estimates of Skilled and Unskilled Labour Placed in Employment Overseas by Employment Exchange

Year	Labourers (Contract)	Domestics (Permanent)	Other Unskilled	Skilled	Total	Unskilled as % of Total
1946	3,111	–	73	287	1,471	91.7
1948	882	–	82	170	1,134	85.0
1949	336	–	28	78	442	82.3
1955	442	109	190	5	746	99.3
1956	645	190	377	570	1,782	68.0
1957	648	117	255	609	1,629	62.6
1958	545	115	118	376	1,154	67.4
1959	740	118	219	558	135	65.9
1960	1,061	181	333	752	2,327	67.6
1961	1,128	91	365	746	2,330	67.9
1962	992	93	535	861	2,481	65.3
1963	1,448	88	298	632	2,466	74.2
1964	1,060	125	431	817	2,433	66.3

Source: Department of Labour, *Annual Reports* (1946–64).

ECONOMIC IMPLICATIONS OF MIGRATION

It is not easy to assess accurately the overall macroeconomic impact of early post-war migration on Barbados. Some authors have attempted to analyse the economic costs of migration to home countries in terms of the loss of skilled manpower. This is the so-called brain drain phenomenon.[6] My analysis looked at the relationship between migration and skills as well as the role of remittances. The available statistical data on Barbadian migration do not support sophisticated cost analyses of the brain drain phenomenon.

Most of the individuals emigrating under the various schemes were highly unskilled. Table 8.2 reveals that the proportion of unskilled migrants was quite high during the years immediately following World War II, but fell sharply after 1955. Most migrants were labourers on contract to the United States and domestics whose status became permanent after a specified period of service, which was usually one year. Between 1956 and 1964, a peak migration period, the absolute number of skilled people migrating rose from 570 in 1956 to 817 in 1964. However, the proportion of skilled migrants averaged in the region of 32.8 percent of total migrants. The Department of Labour has documented that most of the skilled and professional migrants were in occupations such as carpentry, motor mechanics, dressmaking, nursing, teaching and

Table 8.3
Value of Remittances from Overseas

Category	1946–56	1957–59	1960–62	1963–65	1969–71	1972–75
Total remittances ($m)	1.4	3.9	5.6	6.1	6.6	9.3
Remittances as % of imports	–	5.8	7.4	6.8	3.2	2.8
Remittances as % of exports	–	9.6	15.4	12.6	11.4	9.0

Source: Department of Labour, *Annual Reports* (1957–75).

engineering. It is also noteworthy that a large proportion of the skilled people emigrated to England on a permanent basis. The majority of labourers went to the United States on contract. It is reasonable to argue that the economy suffered a permanent loss of skills through migration, especially to England.

Palmer (1979) has presented data to show that there was a loss of skills through migration from Barbados to the United States, stating that between 1967 and 1976, 16,413 people migrated to that country. Of this amount, 1,407 or 8.6 percent were skilled and professional migrants. In this skilled group 42.2 percent were in medical and related fields, and 75 percent in these fields were nurses. A comparison with other Caribbean countries for the same period reveals that the proportions of skilled and professional workers were 7.6 percent in Jamaica, 6.7 percent in Trinidad and 10.4 percent in Guyana. Thus, the Barbados rate of skilled migration to the United States was slightly higher than that of Jamaica and Trinidad. These proportions seem relatively low at first glance. However, in a small economy like Barbados where skills were in very scarce supply, the number of skilled emigrants represented a severe loss of human capital to the economy.

Remittances are a benefit to Barbados because they constitute foreign exchange inflow into the economy. Table 8.3 shows that the economy benefited from remittances in absolute terms particularly between 1957 and 1975. However, the absolute value of remittances cannot tell us much about the importance of these inflows over time. Following Ecevit and Zachariah (1978), we related remittances to the value of imports and exports. Table 8.3 shows that this ratio fell between 1962 and 1975. However, later balance-of-payments data indicate that the value of remittances rose from $35.3 million in 1987 to $168.3 million in 2000. (See *Balance of Payments of Barbados 2002*, published by the Central Bank of Barbados.) In the year 2000 the ratio of remittances to imports was 8.2 percent compared with 2.8 percent in the period 1972–75. One can argue that the

Table 8.4
Remittances from the Contract Farm Labour Scheme

Year	Workers Recruited	Remittances Received ('000)
1976	1,696	1,057
1978	1,326	972
1980	1,578	1,428
1982	1,258	1,113
1984	1,033	1,250
1985	1,077	1,311
1987	999	1,269
1995	662	1,110
1997	636	951
1999	565	940

Source: Department of Labour, *Barbados Annual Reports* (1976–99).

relative ability of foreign exchange from remittances to pay for imports between 1960 and 1975 declined with a falling rate of migration. However, it can be hypothesized that remittances rose thereafter because the incomes of migrants expanded in the host country.

It is, however, difficult to calculate the direct impact of remittances on economic growth and development. Ecevit and Zachariah (1978) assert that remittances are transfers of income for personal consumption by the immediate family of the worker, and need not be channelled into productive investment. Therefore, although the primary balance-of-payments effect of remittances is likely to be positive, the impact on economic growth may be negative, especially if the remittances are spent on consumer imports.

It is also useful to examine remittances associated with the contract farm labour scheme to the United States and Canada. The Canadian scheme continues up to the present. Table 8.4 shows that the remittances from these schemes fell during the 1990s, as a result of the cessation of the United States' contract farm labour programme in the early 1990s. Remittances were compulsory savings deducted from the wages of workers at the rate of 23 percent of the wages of farm workers in the United States scheme, and 25 percent in the case of labourers contracted under the Canadian scheme.

THE SECTORAL DISTRIBUTION OF LABOUR

The period of colonial development (1946–60) shows the following labour resource allocation patterns.

1. A continued high proportion of the labour force employed in agriculture, although there was an absolute fall in agricultural employment;
2. A decline in sectoral working population participation rates;
3. A decline of employment in the traditional manufacturing sector both in terms of absolute numbers and as a proportion of the employed labour force;
4. A decline in the traditional services sector (domestic servants, petty trades, etc.) and a shift to other higher productivity employment in commerce, finance and the civil service.

The 1946 Population Census documents that 29.6 percent of the "gainfully occupied" population were involved in primary pursuits, 20 percent in "manufacturing and repair" and 23 percent in "other services". It is important to discuss the composition of the last two of these major categories. In the category "manufacturing and repair" most of the gainfully employed were involved in areas such as sugar milling, dressmaking and other small craft, garage and metal work related to sugar factory operations. Thus, the contribution of this sector to employment is not a measure of industrialization in the modern sense. In the category "other services", 15.6 percent of the total gainfully employed worked in domestic services.

Cumper's (1959) analysis for the period 1954–55 reveals changes in sectoral employment patterns in the male and female labour force. The percentage of men and women employed in primary occupations remained high despite slight changes. He shows that employment in primary occupations accounted for 28.6 percent of the male labour force in 1955 compared to 31.1 percent in 1946. In the female labour force, primary labour rose slightly from 26.8 percent in 1946 to 27.5 percent in 1955. His most important finding was a decline in the proportion of women involved in service occupations. The proportion of the female labour force in the last category declined from 32.6 percent in 1946 to 24.3 percent in 1955. This was primarily due to a drop in employment in domestic services and dressmaking because of emigration or voluntary withdrawal from the labour force. Despite these changes employment in primary occupations was still a dominant feature of the period 1946–55.

The 1960 census shows a 2.7 percent fall in the proportion of people in the employed labour force involved in primary occupations. There was also a sharp drop in the actual number of people employed in primary occupations from 27,100 in 1946 to 22,900 in 1960. In this same year the proportion of the employed labour force in services increased over the 1946 level.

The intercensal period 1946–60 was, however, characterized by a decline in sectoral working population participation rates. The participation rate is the number of persons engaged in the economic activity, as a proportion of the population fifteen years old and over. Harewood's (1972) study attempted to measure the relative importance of the demand for and supply of labour as contributing to the intercensal decline in economic activity participation in the Eastern Caribbean. He found that in Barbados the general participation rate for males in agriculture declined by 6.5 percent points while for women the drop was 3.9 percent points. This decline in participation rates in agriculture is related to the 15.5 percent fall in the actual number of people employed in agriculture.

Harewood attributes the decline in agricultural employment between 1946 and 1960 to a contraction in the demand for agricultural labour because of an increase in labour-saving machinery in the sugar industry. He argues also that mechanization might have resulted from a reduced supply of labour. About two-thirds of the fall in agricultural employment was attributable to lower labour demand, and one-third to a reduction in the supply of labour. In traditional manufacturing activities, the decline in participation rates for males was 5.0 percent and for females 4.8 percent. The overall fall in the number of people employed in manufacturing was 5,300. The loss in jobs was among small cottage industries and small-scale units, for example, tailors, shoemakers and dressmakers. With the rise in factory industrialization, jobs were destroyed in this traditional small-scale manufacturing sector. Part of the reduction was also due to the emigration discussed above. Harewood's study also shows a drop in participation rates in services by 1.2 percent among males, and 3.9 percent among females. This was primarily attributable to a contraction in the number of domestic servants from 11,700 in 1946 to 8,000 in 1960. Large-scale emigration was also a cause of these developments.

One limitation of our analysis is that the results of the 1946 census, which was carried out using a method designed to estimate the "gainfully occupied", are not strictly comparable with the results of the 1960 and 1970 censuses, which used the labour force method. The 1946 census distinguished between the "gainfully occupied" and "not gainfully occupied". The "gainfully occupied" were all persons engaged in an occupation that brought in money. The 1960 census defined the labour force as persons ten years and over who were not attending school. The 1970 census covered persons fourteen years and over. These differences blur the labour force statistics considerably. (See Abdulah 1977.)

The 1966 survey data showed a high proportion of people in primary occupations (see Table 8.5). The data reveal a large drop in manufacturing employment, but this is to be expected, as many traditional occupations declined rapidly. Further, if we exclude sugar milling, employment in the manufacturing sector in 1966 can be estimated at 7,400 or 9.2 percent of the employed labour force. The statistics on manufacturing in the post-1960 period cannot be compared with data for the period 1946–60.

Table 8.5
Sectoral Distribution of Employed Labour Force (Percent)

Sector	1960	1966	1970	1980	1985	1991	2000
Agriculture	26.4	28.1	17.7	9.2	6.5	5.7	3.8
Mining and quarrying	0.6	0.2	–	0.2	0.2	–	–
Manufacturing	15.3	10.9	13.8[a]	15.0	12.0	10.0	8.0
Construction	10.6	9.5	12.8	8.0	8.0	9.0[b]	10.9[b]
Public utilities	0.9	1.4	–	0.9	2.7	1.6	1.5
Commerce	17.3	17.6	18.2	20.8	22.0	15.5	14.8
Transport and communications	5.2	6.3	6.8[c]	5.9	5.6	4.6	3.9
Other services	23.7	26.0	30.7	40.0	43.0	53.6	57.1
Total	100.0	100.0	100.0	100.0	100.0	100.0	100.0

[a] Includes mining and sugar milling.
[b] Includes quarrying.
[c] Includes public utilities.

Sources: Population Census (1960, 1970); *Labour Force Survey* (1966); Central Bank of Barbados, *Annual Statistical Digest* (2002); Central Bank of Barbados, *Barbados Development Plan* (1979–83).

Employment levels in commerce and services remained high in relation to the total labour force.

Table 8.5 indicates the sharp increase in commerce and other services after 1966. In 1970, commerce (distribution and finance) employed 18.2 percent of the working labour force. This high proportion of the labour force in commerce is related to the import orientation of the economy and the rapid expansion of financial institutions such as banks and insurance companies during the 1970s. The proportion of the employed labour force in other services rose to 43.0 percent by 1985 and 57.0 percent in 2000. The rapid rise in employment in other services is associated with the growth of tourism and the public sector. The expansion in employment in the public sector was due to increases in public expenditure on education, health and the social services. The public sector has been the highest employer of labour since 1991. The category "other services" includes tourism, finance and business services.

Craigwell and Warner (2003) report an increase in the overall participation rate in Barbados from 64.7 percent in 1981 to 68.55 percent in 2000. There was a slight fall in the participation rate for men from 77.2 percent in 1981 to 74.7 percent in 2000. The rate rose for women from 54.0 percent to 62.8 percent over the same period. According to Coppin (1995), the rise in the female participation rate reflected better educational facilities and the expansion of services. Craigwell and Warner (2003) also suggest that many of the new jobs after 1981 seem to have been secured by new entrants to the labour force, rather than workers released from manufacturing and agriculture. There was a higher level of educated workers with secondary and tertiary education.

FEMALE EMPLOYMENT AND PARTICIPATION

We need to comment further on the female participation rate mentioned briefly in the previous paragraph. The main evaluative studies of female occupation in Barbados after 1946 are Lynch (1995), Coppin (1995) and Craigwell and Warner (2003). Lynch documents the decline in female participation between 1946 and 1980, from 58.7 percent to 54.1 percent. This decline was due mainly to external migration and longer time spent in school. The most important aspect of female participation during this period was the "feminization" of clerical labour as the economy became more service oriented. The percentage of females in clerical work rose from 30.9 percent in 1946 to 63.3 percent in 1980. Also, the percentage of women in managerial and administrative activities rose from 2.3 percent in 1946 to 18.6 percent in 1980.

The salient feature of female participation in the Barbadian labour market after 1980 as noted by Craigwell and Warner (2003) was the rapid rise in participation in the female age group between thirty-five and forty years of age, from 73.8 percent in 1981 to 88.6 percent by 2000. A large section of this group worked in banking, financial services and communications. There was also continued "feminization" of clerical and service occupations. The rapid growth of the public service also led to an expansion of a wide range of clerical and professional opportunities available to women.

HUMAN RESOURCE DEVELOPMENT

Barbadian governments have shown a commitment to human resource development as a fundamental aspect of development policy. Our focus here is the provision of education and health services. The principal rationale for expenditure on education stems from the need to provide human capital. Development requires adequate supplies of high-level man power, doctors, agronomists and so fourth, as well as sub-professional and technical personnel. Education contributes to national productivity as well as personal development, since it increases the earning capacity of the individual. The main constraint on the development of human resources is the problem of absorptive capacity, which relates to the maximum number of persons who can be employed without redundancy or serious underutilization of skills.

The most significant aspect of educational development in Barbados after 1960 is the provision of free education at the point of delivery up to university level. Bishop, Corbin and Duncan (1998) have discussed some of the major developments in education, including the abolition of tuition fees in government secondary schools, financial assistance by government to approved independent secondary schools, subsidized school meals, and the textbook loan scheme.

One of the most serious challenges facing the Barbadian government is increasing and retaining the educational output at the tertiary level. The per capita cost is highest at the university level and must be financed by taxation or borrowing. Finance is a constraint on the expansion of the university plant, although there is a need to expand enrolments in science and technology. Some independent observers have justifiably argued that Barbadian university students at the Cave Hill campus should contribute towards the cost of their university education, in an increasingly competitive educational environment.

Health care improvements should also increase labour productivity, which is a function of a large number of variables, including management, education, attitudes about work, and so forth. A healthy labour force is likely to increase output by spending more hours on the job than an unhealthy labour force. After 1960 the establishment of polyclinics supplemented the provision of health care at the Queen Elizabeth Hospital. The establishment of these clinics was an important step in decentralizing medical care in Barbados. Comprehensive maternal and child health programmes were also available at the polyclinics.

After 1980 the upgrading of dental services and the expansion of the national drug service, which provides drugs for certain chronic illnesses free of charge, were important objectives of the national health budget. The HIV/AIDS prevention programme has evolved over time. HIV/AIDS is a major health threat to workers in the twenty to forty-five age group. Public provision of health care in Barbados has been well complemented by private enterprise in general practitioner and specialist services.

UNEMPLOYMENT IN BARBADOS

Unemployment in Barbados has always been a problem in spite of structural change, human resource development and slower population growth. Table 8.6 shows the level of unemployment between 1946 and 2000. Unemployment in 1946 was 7.8 percent. However, there was considerable disguised and seasonal unemployment during this period, so that a single unemployment rate is doubtful.

The high levels of unemployment after 1970 are explained by the 1973–74 oil crisis and the recession in the world economy of 1980–81. The period 1970–76 was marked by a rapid expansion of the labour force. The economic recession caused by the oil crisis of 1973 led to stagflationary conditions, and the economy was unable to absorb the additions to the labour force (Table 8.6). The growth in the economy between 1976 and

Table 8.6
Unemployment

Year	Labour Force ('000)	Unemployed ('000)	Unemployed as % of Labour Force
1946	93.7	7.3	7.8
1955	89.0	–	–
1960	92.2	7.2	7.8
1966	93.3	12.2	13.2
1970	92.6	9.0	9.7
1976	104.1	16.2	15.6
1980	114.8	14.5	12.6
1983	112.6	16.9	15.0
1984	112.3	19.2	17.1
1985	113.3	21.2	18.7
1987	128.0	22.8	17.8
1991	129.6	22.5	17.3
1995	137.0	26.9	19.6
1998	138.6	16.9	12.2
2000	142.3	13.3	9.4

Sources: Census of Population (1946, 1960, 1970); Labour Force Surveys (1955, 1966); Economic Report (1987); Central Bank of Barbados, Annual Statistical Digest (2002).

1980 led to a decline in unemployment so that by 1980 the rate stood at 12.6 percent. Thereafter the rate rose sharply during the first half of the 1980s as the economy tried to deal with recession. High unemployment persisted up to 1995 and was exacerbated by the recession of 1991 (see Chapter 11).

The analysis shows that between 1976 and 1995 unemployment remained a serious problem, despite the economic policies. The reasons are rooted in the dynamic of the labour surplus economy. First, the problem of labour surplus after 1946 was worsened by the expansion of capital-intensive modes of production in the primary and secondary sectors. Second, because the economy remained dependent on metropolitan decision making, levels of unemployment tended to fluctuate with economic changes in the industrial economies. Third, during the 1960s, appropriate reforms in the educational system were not implemented to provide a level of indigenous managerial, technical and marketing skills to exploit the productive capabilities of the economy. Fourth, the rate of growth of skilled labour was a slow process, but the government's institution of skills training and the establishment of the Samuel Jackman Prescod Polytechnic helped to relieve this bottleneck in the 1980s and 1990s.

Finally, improved investor confidence and efficient management of the fiscal and balance-of-payments deficits reduced unemployment in the second half of the 1990s. The major problem facing Barbadian policy-makers in their efforts to reduce unemployment is to improve the economy's international competitiveness in the face of trade liberalization.

SUMMARY

The reallocation of labour in the economy of Barbados was due to the diversification of the economy away from sugar. However, the earliest policy initiative to deal with the labour surplus was the encouragement of external migration, mainly to the United Kingdom, the United States and Canada. The early migrants were primarily unskilled, but there is reason to believe that the rate of skilled migration increased after 1960 as immigration regulations in these countries became more stringent.

My analysis showed that by 2000 the service sector absorbed the largest proportion of the labour force. The reallocation of labour to service activities reflects the strong influence of external trade and distribution and the philosophy of public sector involvement in the economy. Manufacturing was only a moderate employer of labour during the period. Unemployment remained high but declined after 1995 as the economy recovered from the recession of 1991.

9
CHAPTER

The External Sector

COLONIALISM, SIZE AND OPENNESS

In Chapter 2, the view was expressed that the small system is an open system. The implication of this argument is that openness (measured by a high ratio of external transactions to monetary GDP) is a manifestation of size and dependence. The purpose of this chapter is to show how, in the case of Barbados, dependence was reflected in the behaviour of the external sector. We are interested in the impact of colonial trade relations, size and structural changes on trade flows, as well as the behaviour of exogenous variables such as the terms of trade, the capacity to import, and the import surplus or current account on the balance of payments.

Our early proposition was that colonialism provided the initial conditions that led to a pattern of trade in which the economy was dominated by the plantation system. Dependence on trade is not, therefore, an exclusive function of size. Although Demas (1965) placed emphasis on size, he also recognized that trade dependence was a multidimensional phenomenon. He stipulated that a colonial economic structure makes for a high dependence on foreign trade, irrespective of the size of the country.

The colonial history of Barbados is perhaps the most important determinant of the heavy commodity concentration in sugar exports as well as the geographic concentration on the United Kingdom market during the early post-war period. Many physically large ex-colonial developing economies had similar patterns of export commodity concentration. These patterns persisted because the system of preferences instituted by the former colonizing powers meant that the ex-colonies enjoyed the protection of sheltered markets.

The relationship between size and external trade has been tested empirically by a number of authors, including Kuznets (1963), Carter (1997) and Khalaf (1976). Using cross-sectional data, Kuznets found that small countries are relatively more dependent on foreign trade than are larger countries. The literature has also given support to the view that small countries tend to concentrate their exports in a few markets. However, the empirical literature has not demonstrated conclusively the relative weights of size and structural change or "degree of development" as determinants of foreign trade concentration. Further, the empirical tests of the size/openness hypothesis have largely ignored the impact of the colonial experience.

The ratio of external trade to GDP has always been high in Barbados, but has fallen in recent times. The ratio of imports to GDP averaged over 70 percent for the period between 1950 and 1975. Between 1975 and 1985, the average import ratio fell to around 65 percent and reached 53.9 percent by 2000. Because small size also restricts the development of the capital goods sector, we should also expect a high ratio of imports of capital goods to domestic capital formation. In Barbados this ratio averaged 58 percent between 1975 and 1985, but fell to 42.2 percent by 2000.

EXPORTS OF VISIBLE GOODS AND SERVICES

My analysis is now concerned with the impact of structural change on the exports of visible goods and services. The two most important developments influencing export diversification were a decline in sugar monoculture, the rise of the electronics export sector, and the strong performance of services exports. As shown in Table 9.1, the period of sharp adjustment in the export sector in Barbados was between 1965 and 1980. The decline in monoculture was followed by a sharp fall in the ratio of sugar exports, to total exports, from 77.7 percent in 1965 to 36.0 percent in 1980. Despite this decline, it should be noted that sugar remained the most important foreign exchange earner in the visible trade up to 1980.

The export diversification programme placed considerable emphasis on the export of electronics components for the US market. Clothing was also identified as a viable export commodity. The enclave type of export

Table 9.1
Percent Composition of Barbadian Exports

Category	1965	1970	1980	1990	2000
Sugar and molasses	77.7	55.5	36.0	26.5	13.8
Rum	5.8	5.2	1.0	5.9	6.4
Other food and beverages	5.1	3.6	4.2	9.8	15.6
Chemicals	0.4	3.4	6.4	15.8	12.5
Electrical components	–	10.3	18.8	10.9	11.3
Clothing	0.7	5.9	14.6	6.0	1.5
Other manufactures	3.5	8.8	18.5	24.6	25.0
All other	6.8	7.3	0.5	0.5	13.9
Total	100.0	100.0	100.0	100.0	100.0

Source: Central Bank of Barbados, *Annual Statistical Digest* (2002).

Table 9.2
Direction of Exports (Percent of Total)

Year	United Kingdom	United States	Canada	CARICOM	All Other
1960	61.3	2.9	11.2	18.3	6.1
1965	42.1	10.4	7.8	14.8	24.9
1970	38.6	18.3	4.6	21.1	15.3
1980	6.6	36.3	4.0	27.8	25.3
1985	5.7	51.8	1.4	22.6	18.5
1990	18.2	13.0	2.9	30.7	35.2
2000	13.0	15.3	2.0	42.0	27.7

Source: Central Bank of Barbados, *Annual Statistical Digest* (2002).

promotion led to a high degree of geographic concentration of manufacturing exports after 1970. The main export markets were the United States and CARICOM.

The foreign exchange earning capacity of Barbados after 1980 was heavily dependent on the export of services, comprising mainly tourism services. Services exports expanded from $611.9 million in 1987 to $1.2 billion in 2000, about twice the amount of visible exports. Our analysis of the import surplus will also capture the importance of services.

Table 9.2 shows the direction of exports. The trends are as follows: the decline in the proportion of exports to the United Kingdom; the rise and fall of the US market; the insignificance of the Canadian market; the strong growth of exports to CARICOM, and the importance of exports to the rest of the world. The decline of the UK market is associated with the fall in sugar exports between 1970 and 1985. During the same period there was a significant rise in the export of electronics components to the United States. The closure of the Intel Corporation in Barbados along with international competition led to the decline in the export of electronics components to the United States after 1985. By the year 2000, the CARICOM market was the largest export market.

STRUCTURAL CHANGE AND IMPORT STRUCTURE

Our examination of import structure is informed by a previous pattern of analysis done by Adams (1967, 1971). During the process of industrialization, one should expect a number of changes in the composition of imports. These include a rise in the share of capital goods imported because of the limitations of the resource base. Second, the share of intermediate goods is also likely to rise, especially in the case of import substitutive industrialization. Further, intermediate imports are necessary to service enclave industries. In his study of developing countries, Adams found that there

Table 9.3
Retained Imports by Economic Category (Percent Composition)

Category	1960	1970	1980	1990	2000
Food and beverages	27.1	21.8	17.6	16.9	14.9
Other consumer goods	16.2	22.9	19.2	20.2	26.3
Intermediate goods	39.0	34.8	46.3	38.7	37.8
Capital goods	14.5	17.7	17.2	22.0	20.8
Unclassified goods	3.2	2.8	-0.3	2.1	0.2
Total	100.0	100.0	100.0	100.0	100.0

Source: Central Bank of Barbados, *Annual Statistical Digest* (2002).

was no association evident for capital goods, but the share of intermediate goods tends to rise. Further, Adams's empirical analysis shows that as industrialization proceeded, the share of manufactured consumer goods fell for the countries under investigation. In his work on Jamaica, Adams observed constancy in the share of food imports over time.

Our analysis of imports in Table 9.3 reveals a number of important tendencies. Overall, intermediate goods constitute the highest proportion of imports. This feature in the early 1960s is related to initial industrialization efforts and the emphasis on import substitution. The proportion of intermediate goods peaked at 46.3 percent in 1980, largely as a result of the expansion of the tourism plant.

The rise in the share of capital goods fulfilled our expectations. The share of capital goods averaged 11 percent for the early years of the 1960s. The tendency for the proportion of capital goods to rise in the late 1960s reflects the boom in hotel building, which increased the demand for both machinery and construction materials. The rise in the importance of capital goods is also explained by expenditures on public goods such as education, transport and housing. By the year 2000, capital goods imported were 20.8 percent of imports.

The share of food and beverage imports declined from 27.1 percent in 1960 to 14.9 percent in 2000 (Table 9.3). This phenomenon may be explained by the inelasticity of the demand for food imports with rising incomes. Cox and Worrell (1978) found that food imports had a low income elasticity of 0.63.

However, paradoxically, Barbados has not really reduced its dependence on imported food. In order to examine dependence we need to look at the ratio of nominal food imports to total food supplies. Only then can we gauge the degree of import substitution in domestic agriculture. A study by the Food and Agricultural Organization (FAO) (1978) found that the ratio of total food imports to total agricultural supplies for the domestic market averaged 66.3 percent for the period 1960–76. This ratio reflects the inability of the domestic agricultural sector to meet local demand. I also estimated a ratio of total food imports to total agricultural supplies of 72.8 percent for 2000 based on trade and GDP estimates. The economy became more self-sufficient in vegetable production over the survey period, but continued to rely heavily on imported meat, rice, cereals, flour and other processed products.

The UK and Canadian markets have declined significantly since 1960. There has been a shift in geographic concentration to the US and CARI-COM markets. By 2000, the United States was the largest supplier of imports to Barbados.

THE COMMODITY TERMS OF TRADE

The commodity terms of trade (Px/Pm) have a significant influence on the capacity to import and on the overall balance of payments. Previous analyses of the Barbadian terms of trade have been carried out by Gafar (1974) for the period 1954–70, based on export/import price indices developed by Gafar and Joefield-Napier (1978). Another study by Codrington and Holder (1984) compared movements in the Barbados terms of trade with those of Trinidad and Tobago. These studies noted that the Barbadian economy experienced a worsening of its commodity terms of trade between 1954 and 1970. Our analysis therefore identifies briefly the main factors affecting this deterioration in the terms of trade index from 198.6 in 1955 to 88.9 in 1980. I was unable to find an officially published export price index for Barbados for the period after 1980. Straughn (2000) compiled an export price index for Barbados. However, he advised caution in the use of this index since he seemed to have doubts about its methodology. I decided not to use this index to examine the terms of trade between 1980 and 2000, because of the problem of comparing Straughn's figures with those of Joefield-Napier for an earlier time period.

An important reason for terms of trade deterioration is the behaviour of the price of sugar. Particularly significant was the slowing after 1963 in the rate of growth of the price of sugar under the Commonwealth Sugar Agreement (CSA). Persaud (1973) showed that the CSA negotiated price of sugar rose by 12 percent between 1954 and 1963 compared with an increase of only 3 percent between 1963 and 1970. This slow-down was related to a fall in the world market price of sugar, which influenced Barbadian sales on the free market.

The commodity terms of trade deteriorated sharply and persistently in Barbados between 1970 and 1980. The overall decline is explained primarily by rapid increases in the price of petroleum products, especially after 1973. The annual average increase in the price of petroleum was 24.9 percent for the period 1969–73, and 40.1 percent for the period 1973–78.

THE CAPACITY TO IMPORT

The deterioration in the terms of trade described above meant that the purchasing power of Barbadian citizens over goods and services from the rest of the world could not be met from merchandise exports. However, the terms of trade concept does not say much about the "capacity to import" in a services economy dependent on tourism and other "invisibles", as well as capital inflows. My definition of the capacity to import follows closely that of Maizels (1968). It is defined as the purchasing power over imports of the foreign exchange derived from exports of goods and services, net transfers and net capital inflows. Further, the capacity to import excludes all short-term capital flows, and short-term monetary movements whether private or official. The concept is defined as follows:

$$Z = 1/Pm \ (X + Xs + N + F)$$

Where
Z = capacity to import
Pm = import price index
X = merchandise exports
Xs = exports of services
N = net transfers
F = long-term net capital inflows

The capacity to import was calculated for the period after the 1973–74 oil crisis using the import deflator 1980 = 100. Table 9.4 shows that the capacity to import grew at an average annual rate of 7.5 percent for the period 1975–80, and a much lower rate of 4 percent for 1980–85, with deterioration in 1981 and 1982. These two years were characterized by recession in the domestic economy. The capacity to import stabilized between 1985 and 1990. I was unable to estimate the capacity to import after 1990 because there are no data on the import price index after this year. The capacity to import signifies that even though a country may be experiencing terms-of-trade deterioration, living standards can be maintained by other inflows of foreign exchange.

THE IMPORT SURPLUS

This section looks at the behaviour of the import surplus or the current account deficit. The import surplus as a ratio of gross domestic investment or GDP can be used to gauge whether the need for external financing has increased or declined over time. The higher this ratio, the greater the country's reliance on foreign borrowing to finance imports. This approach follows the work of Grassman (1980) and Little, Scitovsky and Scott (1970). I examined the period 1970–2000.

Table 9.4
Capacity to Import

Year	Capacity to Import ($m)
1975	753.3
1976	709.8
1977	809.7
1978	870.2
1979	1,040.4
1980	1,063.9
1981	1,014.7
1982	991.8
1983	1,106.7
1984	1,231.8
1985	1,279.9
1987	1,163.1
1988	1,298.9
1989	1,270.5
1990	1,400.7

Source: Central Bank of Barbados, *Annual Statistical Digest* (1987, 2002).

The analysis in Table 9.5 reveals that the need for external financing fell sharply between 1970 and 2000. There was a downward trend in the import surplus as a percent of gross domestic capital formation as well as GDP. The trend is due primarily to the rapid growth of invisibles, chiefly tourism earnings, in the current account. Prior to 1974 the dependence on external resources was much higher, reaching a peak of 28.9 percent of GDP in 1970. Net resources from abroad to finance domestic capital formation were highest between 1973 and 1975. Much of this inflow was in the form of high-priced Eurodollar loans. During the year 2000, a large current account deficit increased the need for external borrowing.

IMPACT OF TRADE LIBERALIZATION

It is difficult to analyse the impact of trade liberalization on the Barbadian economy, because this policy was only introduced in the 1990s, as part of the structural adjustment programme. There is insufficient time series data to perform rigorous economic analysis. However, studies by the Ministry of Agriculture, Barbados as well as Lewis-Bynoe et al. (2000) allow us to draw some tentative conclusions.

Reports by the Barbados Ministry of Agriculture (2002a, 2002b, 2002c) suggest that trade liberalization negatively affected agriculture, especially

Table 9.5
Indicators of External Financial Dependence

Year	Import Surplus $m	Import Surplus as % of GDCF	Import Surplus as % of GDP
1970	83.7	NA	28.9
1971	69.3	NA	21.5
1972	82.9	NA	19.4
1973	102.4	NA	24.0
1974	98.4	58.1	15.3
1975	83.7	53.6	11.9
1978	62.9	24.7	6.7
1980	54.2	14.2	3.7
1985	–81.0	–21.8	–3.7
1990	15.6	2.4	0.5
1995	–87.2	–15.3	–2.8
2000	289.9	30.6	6.8

Note: GDCF = Gross domestic capital formation; NA = not available.

Source: Central Bank of Barbados, Annual Statistical Digest (various years).

the poultry and pork industries, and vegetable production. In the 1990s, in keeping with CARICOM commitments, Barbados removed the requirement for import licences from CARICOM member states, and agricultural products were free to move into Barbados. The WTO Agreement on Agriculture also reinforced trade liberalization. In April 2000, the restrictive licensing regime for sensitive agricultural products was removed and replaced by a tariff regime in which the appropriate bound rate of duty was the only barrier. The bound rate of duty was to be progressively reduced up to 2004.

According to the Barbados Ministry of Agriculture (2002a:13–15), the removal of licences on CARICOM states led to an increase in imports of poultry, which caused some displacement of local production. Imports of pork also increased, leading to a fall in pork production during the late 1990s.

Lewis-Bynoe et al. (2000) assessed the likely impact of the new bound rates. These rates were higher than the old Common External Tariff (CET) rate, thereby offering a measure of protection to industry and agriculture, but caused a rise in the import prices of the products used in these sectors. However, when the rates were reduced to reach WTO ceilings by 2004, the prices of some locally produced goods were higher than their import equivalent. The "tariffication" of trade was intended to be more transparent than the non-tariff barriers. The WTO maintained that tariffication would be gradually reduced until there was a completely liberalized trade environment.

THE CARICOM SINGLE MARKET AND ECONOMY AND THE FREE TRADE AREA OF THE AMERICAS

The CARICOM Single Market and Economy (CSME) has implications for the Barbadian economy. Space constraints do not allow an extensive discussion of the CSME. Further, Caribbean governments planned to implement the CSME after 2000. In 1989 the CARICOM heads of governments met at Grand Anse, Grenada and decided to work towards the CSME. By 1992 the form of the CSME was conceptualized and approved by the heads of government. Essentially the CSME is the regional response to globalization by extending CARICOM. The CSME includes new areas such as the free movement of services, the free movement of factors of production, and the right of establishment and monetary union. The 1973 Treaty of Chaguramus, which created CARICOM, was extended to include nine protocols relating to trade, agriculture, industry, services, transport, competition policy, institutions, disadvantaged countries and disputes settlement. A Caribbean Court of Justice was invested with the powers to interpret the legal provisions of the CSME.

The CSME requires coordinated economic and monetary policies, extensive legislative changes and the creation of new executive instruments and institutions. These changes are necessary to harmonize the financial sectors, customs and fiscal policies, and to facilitate the movement of money and capital. Such extensive reforms imply that each government cannot maintain full national sovereignty. Countries must also be willing to allow free movement of labour. It is also hoped that Barbados will be able to exploit its comparative advantage in services.

The matter of a common currency was taken off the CSME agenda because the conditions of macroeconomic stability do not exist. However, a single market and single economy are really not possible without a single currency. A single economy requires a unified currency to reduce transactions costs and facilitate capital flows in the region.

Despite the constraints on its implementation, the CSME could increase output, broaden the regional market, improve access to international markets and enhance the competitiveness of regional products. However, perhaps too much is expected from the CSME in a region where political leaders have found it difficult to agree on other matters less complex than this stage of regional integration.

The Free Trade Area of the Americas (FTAA) is designed as a free trade area involving thirty-four countries in the Western Hemisphere. Its proposed implementation is December 2005. The Regional Negotiation machinery is the chief instrument advancing strategies for CARICOM members in their negotiations for the FTAA.

FTAA will impact significantly on Barbados and other CARICOM countries. Barbados needs to be able to produce high quality goods to be competitive in this arrangement. One area is services. However, our firms are too small to take advantage of some of the opportunities presented by FTAA. Our manufacturing industries also lack international competitiveness. FTAA, when implemented, will force CARICOM countries to increase their productive efficiency. FTAA will also provide a larger market for our goods, and greater bargaining power with the rest of the world.

FOREIGN DIRECT INVESTMENT (FDI)

The purpose of this brief section is to examine the money value of net FDI in Barbados compared with other CARICOM countries. Early work by Codrington (1987) gives some idea of the importance of FDI in Barbados. Codrington found that in 1985, FDI was highest for the oil companies, followed by manufacturing, insurance and hotels. We have already examined the degree of foreign ownership of hotels and manufacturing establishments in Chapters 6 and 7.

The net nominal amount of FDI received by Barbados relative to other Caribbean countries is shown in Table 9.6. Trinidad and Tobago recorded the most FDI, followed by Jamaica. Barbados averaged only US $11.73 million per annum for the period 1988–98.

Table 9.6
Net FDI in the Caribbean (US $million)

Year	Trinidad & Tobago	Jamaica	Guyana	Barbados	OECS
1988	63.0	–12.0	NA	11.0	101.2
1989	148.9	57.1	NA	8.0	142.7
1990	109.4	137.9	NA	11.0	200.8
1991	144.1	133.2	81.2	7.0	180.5
1992	171.0	142.4	152.3	14.0	148.0
1993	372.6	77.9	25.0	9.0	125.3
1994	512.0	130.0	107.0	13.0	161.0
1995	295.7	147.0	74.0	12.0	232.0
1996	356.3	184.0	92.0	13.0	113.0
1997	999.6	203.0	52.0	15.0	182.0
1998	731.9	369.0	47.0	16.0	232.0
Average per annum	354.95	142.68	78.8	11.73	165.32

Note: OECS = Organization of Eastern Caribbean States; NA = not available.

Sources: UNECLAC (1995) for data between 1988 and 1993. Data for 1994 to 1998 for countries other than Trinidad and Tobago are found in CARICOM Secretariat (2000). Data for Trinidad and Tobago between 1994 and 1998 were obtained from the Central Statistical Office and the Central Bank of Trinidad and Tobago, *The Balance of Payments of Trinidad and Tobago* (1996 to 1998).

Table 9.7
FDI as Percent of Gross Domestic Capital Formation in CARICOM

Country	1994	1995	1996	1997
Antigua and Barbuda	15.3	17.3	8.7	15.0
Bahamas	3.8	15.3	14.3	32.7
Barbados	5.6	5.9	6.2	6.9
Belize	12.7	15.6	12.8	9.1
Dominica	31.2	75.9	24.8	27.8
Granada	21.8	23.7	18.9	24.7
Guyana	34.0	26.4	29.7	15.7
Jamaica	9.9	8.9	9.8	12.6
St Kitts and Nevis	18.2	23.6	26.1	32.0
St Lucia	22.2	22.8	16.3	29.1
St Vincent	59.9	35.1	19.5	48.5
Trinidad and Tobago	51.3	36.0	34.9	109.0
Latin America and the Caribbean	9.1	9.4	12.5	16.1
Developing countries	8.0	7.3	8.4	10.2

Sources: UNCTAD, *World Investment Report* (2000); CARICOM Secretariat (2000).

The ratio of net FDI to gross domestic capital formation is a better measure of comparison between the Caribbean territories. This measure shows that Trinidad and Tobago again ranks first, and Barbados has the lowest level of FDI inflows. The Barbados ratio is also below the average for all developing countries (see Table 9.7). The implication is that Barbados depends more on domestic saving and other foreign borrowing to finance development.

SUMMARY

The Barbadian economy achieved a measure of export diversification after 1960. Sugar, chemicals, electronics components and clothing were the main exports. The decline in the sugar industry was reflected in the sharp fall in sugar exports after 1980. Clothing and electronics exports also fell significantly. Barbados's foreign exchange earning capacity was boosted by the rapid development of services, primarily tourism, which led to the strong growth of services exports.

Economic development also caused a rise in the share of intermediate and capital goods imported. This was due primarily to import substitution, which played an important role in trade policy during the period. The analysis also commented on some of the likely effects of trade liberalization.

The terms of trade deteriorated before 1980, but the country's capacity to import grew, mainly as a result of strong inflows of invisibles. The heavy external financial dependence of the economy appears to have fallen when we used the ratio of the import surplus to gross investment and GDP. Although Barbados depends on FDI, the level of FDI inflows was low when compared with the rest of the Caribbean.

10

Financial Intermediation

INTRODUCTION

This chapter discusses financial intermediation in Barbados. We examine the evolution of the monetary system, the relationship between financial structure and development, the degree of savings mobilization achieved by banks, social efficiency of commercial banking, the structure of the financial system in the 1990s and the importance of financial innovation.

Economic development depends on the efficient allocation of funds by financial intermediaries to productive sectors of the economy. Financial intermediaries facilitate the transfer of funds from surplus spending units to deficit spending units. According to Patrick (1966), the more developed financial markets are, the more efficient is the intermediation process. Craigwell, Downes and Howard (2001) found that finance was a causal factor in economic growth in Barbados. The importance of financial intermediation implies that priority of analysis should be given to savings mobilization and social or allocative efficiency. Before analysing financial intermediation, we look briefly at the evolution of the monetary system in which saving and investment took place.

EVOLUTION OF THE MONETARY SYSTEM

The Barbadian monetary system has evolved from a dependent colonial system to a more autonomous central bank system. Between 1946 and 1973 the colonial monetary system in Barbados was an extension of the monetary system of the United Kingdom. The prices of financial assets and exchange rates in Barbados were determined by monetary conditions in the United Kingdom. For example, the Eastern Caribbean Currency Authority was unable to make use of bank rate policy to influence commercial bank interest rates in the territories in which it served. Further, the financial institutions in Barbados were predominantly foreign owned and controlled. Therefore, the Barbadian economy showed all the characteristics of colonial monetary dependence during this period.

The colonial monetary system was designed to facilitate financial settlements resulting from trade between the United Kingdom and its colonies.

The sterling exchange standard meant that the expansion of currency in the colony had to be backed by an inflow of sterling of equivalent value. The colony therefore had no control over its money supply. This was attributable to the free convertibility of currencies and the integration of the colony's money markets with those of the United Kingdom. However, the commercial banks were able to increase the money supply through credit expansion, primarily to the import and export sectors, which were strongly based on sugar.

Foreign ownership and control of financial institutions meant that credit was very often withheld from indigenous entrepreneurs who were productive socially. Foreign bank subsidiaries preferred to lend to expatriate entrepreneurs who faced a smaller risk of loss. In a later section we discuss the lending practices of colonial banks in more detail.

The Central Bank of Barbados was established in 1973, and has the power to create money by lending to government. This facility introduced a new pattern of monetary management. Chapter 11 shows that money creation to finance government budget deficits had a significant influence on the balance of payments. Further, the Central Bank was able to influence commercial bank interest rates and credit expansion by its exercise of monetary policy techniques. This meant that there was a measure of monetary regulation of commercial banks that was not present in the colonial period under the Eastern Caribbean Currency Authority.

The Central Bank also exercised prudential regulation of the commercial banks by means of on-site supervision. Prudential regulation was necessary to protect the banks against systemic risks, by ensuring that the banking system applied certain efficiency criteria in the management of its operations. The Central Bank also acquired the power to change the exchange rate and to determine exchange control regulations. These substantial changes in the monetary system provide the context for understanding the character of financial intermediation, as well as the importance of financial innovation during the survey period. However, the issues in financial regulation are numerous and complex, and cannot be covered adequately in a single chapter. The articles in the Central Bank's publication *Central Banking in Barbados* (Codrington, Craigwell and Haynes 1997) give readers more insight into the issues of monetary policy and regulation.

DEVELOPMENT OF THE FINANCIAL STRUCTURE

Goldsmith (1969) has observed that in the course of economic development, a country's financial superstructure grows more rapidly than its national product and wealth. First, he found that the ratio of total financial assets to national wealth increases during the course of development. Second, he reported that the share of the banking system in the assets of all financial

Table 10.1
Indicators of Financial Development (1960–98) (Percent)

Year	TFA/GDP	ACB/GDP	ANB/GDP	ACB/TFA	ANB/TFA
1960–63	59.2	44.6	14.2	75.7	24.3
1968–71	122.4	83.9	23.8	68.2	19.6
1976–80	121.3	70.6	41.9	54.1	32.1
1984–85	112.6	63.8	43.0	56.6	38.1
1990–94	165.8	80.8	60.4	48.8	36.2
1995–98	183.2	106.5	51.0	59.1	30.0

Source: Central Bank of Barbados, *Annual Statistical Digest* (1980, 1987, 1999).

institutions declines, while the share of non-bank assets increases. We examined whether these relationships held for Barbados, using the GDP in the absence of reliable measures for national wealth. The following ratios were computed:

1. TFA/GDP;
2. ACB/GDP; ANB/GDP
3. ACB/TFA; ANB/TFA

Where
TFA = total assets of the financial system;
ACB = assets of commercial banks;
ANB = assets of non-bank financial institutions.

Table 10.1 shows that the TFA/GDP ratio grew rapidly in the 1960s, stabilized in the 1970s and fell in the 1980s. This indicates that the financial system experienced an early rapid growth relative to the real sector. The period between 1960 and 1980 coincided with the growth of new banking institutions and a general expansion in economic activity led by tourism and other service activities. The performance of the TFA/GDP ratio up to 1980 supports Goldsmith's view that the financial system expands more rapidly than the economic infrastructure during the course of development. Economic recession led to a decline in this ratio during the early 1980s. The financial system also experienced strong growth in the 1990s, as a result of tourism expansion, which increased the demand for loans and deposits.

The commercial banking system was the main contributor to financial intermediation during the entire period, as shown by the performance of the ACB/GDP ratio. The non-bank intermediation sector expanded more slowly. Despite the importance of commercial banking, the share of the banking system in total financial assets actually declined over the entire period, supporting Goldsmith's second observation. This is shown by the fall in the ACB/TFA ratio, and the gentle rise in the ANB/TFA ratio. By 1996 the share of assets of financial institutions was as follows: commercial banks, 56.0 percent; Central Bank, 11.5 percent; life insurance companies, 8.9 percent ; credit unions, 3.8 percent; trust and mortgage companies, 7.2 percent; merchant banks and finance companies, 1.2 percent; and the National Insurance Scheme, 14.4 percent. It should be noted that even though credit union assets are a small percentage of the total assets of the financial system, credit union membership has increased rapidly among middle- and lower-income workers, from 37,586 in 1990 to 69,097 in 1998. (See Central Bank of Barbados, *Annual Statistical Digest*, 1999.)

FINANCIAL DEEPENING

Financial deepening is measured by the increase in the ratio of total bank deposits to GDP or (TD/GDP). Financial deepening shows the ability of the banking system to mobilize financial savings. Financial deepening cannot be explained by the growth of income alone. Further, the importance of the role of institutions, as well as monetary policy in the Barbadian case, reduces the effectiveness of the econometric method in explaining financial deepening. In Barbados, important causes of financial deepening are the growth of branch banking, the impact of the Puerto Rican model, interest rates, and the policies of the Central Bank of Barbados.

A caveat is necessary here. Financial liberalization was not a factor in the process of financial deepening. No significant attempts were made by the Central Bank to liberalize interest rates or to pursue extensive capital account liberalization. There has been, however, gradual relaxation of exchange controls. Therefore, this section does not address the issue of financial liberalization in Barbados, nor analyse the extensive literature on this subject.

Table 10.2 shows financial deepening over time. The ratio was low in the early years because of the low level of incomes and underdevelopment of the banks' branch network. Financial deepening improved during the late 1960s and early 1970s. First, the operation of the Puerto Rican model increased the flow of deposit money by firms into the banking system. It is difficult to quantify this effect, however, as data on deposit ownership only became available after 1973. Further, the income effect of the model would have stimulated the growth of individual deposit holdings.

Second, deposit rate competition also influenced the TD/GDP ratio between 1968 and 1972. Rate-based competition by three newly established American banks was designed to attract depositors away from the more established British and Canadian banks. Actual rates payable on time deposits were negotiable with prospective borrowers. The older

Table 10.2
Financial Deepening (TD/GDP)
(Period Averages)

Period	TD/GDP (%)
1950–54	39.8
1955–59	39.3
1960–64	37.2
1965–69	55.2
1970–74	62.2
1975–79	51.6
1980–85	49.5
1990–95	67.8
1995–2000	91.8

Sources: Central Bank of Barbados, *Annual Report* (1987); Central Bank of Barbados, *Annual Statistical Digest* (2002).

banks responded with both price and non-price competition to protect their own deposit volume. Such competition continued into 1973.

Third, the expansion of the banks' branch network is very important. By 1959 four banks existed in Barbados, with a total of six branches and a branch to population ratio of 1:39,466. Of these six branches, four were located in Bridgetown. The banks were unable to mobilize rural savings. By the end of 1973, forty-one branches were established (see Central Bank of Barbados, *Annual Statistical Digests*, 1980–87). This development helped to mobilize both rural and urban savings. The banks were also able to advertise their financial services on a broader basis.

The TD/GDP ratio declined between 1973 and 1985. This is explained primarily by the rise in the interest rate differential between nominal Eurodollar rates and nominal domestic interest rates, anticipation of exchange controls against sterling, as well as a decline in domestic real deposit rates. Previous work by Howard (1976) and Worrell (1974) shows that the rise in the differential between nominal domestic and nominal external interest rates caused an outflow of funds from Barbados. This was reflected in a slowing in the rate of growth of deposits in Barbados between 1972 and 1973. For instance, in 1973 the London three-month Eurodollar deposit rate rose from 6.6 percent at the beginning of the year to 10.4 percent by September 1973. Further, rates in London ranged from 9 percent to 15 percent depending on the size of the deposit. In the absence of exchange controls against sterling and small commissions on onward transfers of funds, there was considerable incentive for big savers in

Barbados to invest funds abroad in 1973. The actual magnitude of the outflow was not ascertainable.

The anticipation of general exchange controls after the Central Bank was established in 1973 also contributed to the flight of deposits. Despite the free transfers into sterling it was expected that this regime would be amended when the Barbadian currency was issued toward the end of 1973. Individuals apparently invested funds abroad to escape the possibility of close monitoring by the exchange control authority. There was also a fear of devaluation just before the Barbados dollar was issued (see the Central Bank of Barbados *Annual Report*, 1973). Further, a few commercial banks reported that some firms held funds abroad which were earmarked for local investments because of the uncertainty surrounding the parity of the new Barbadian dollar.

The fall in real deposit rates in Barbados is equally important in explaining the outflow of funds. The real deposit rate is the difference between the nominal deposit rate and the rate of inflation. Following Chandavarkar (1971) and Galbis (1979) and building on Howard (1976), we contend that negative real domestic interest rates suggest a measure of "financial repression" and the inappropriateness of deposit rate policy. In times of inflation the nominal interest rate is not a good indicator of the yield on savings instruments. Howard (1976) found that the rapid decline in real yields, particularly between 1972 and 1974, was one of the most important factors explaining the fall in real deposits and the decline in the TD/GDP ratio after 1974.

The analysis for the period after 1973 emphasized the interest rate differential between London and Barbados and the real interest rate in explaining the behaviour of deposits. However, Howard (1979b) has shown in a separate study on the demand for money that the nominal interest rate was not a statistically significant variable influencing the public's preference for real time deposits between 1960 and 1976. Further, most of the variation in real financial savings was due more to variations in real income than to nominal deposit rate movements. Prior to 1973, despite some deposit rate competition, there was no sharp upward movement in the level of nominal deposit rates. This stability influenced the regression analysis, which captured most of the period prior to 1973. The regression results do not invalidate our explanations of real deposit changes for the period after 1973. Even though Worrell (1982) found a statistically insignificant relationship between nominal deposits and real deposit rates, it should be remembered that price expectations and real interest rates may not have played as important a role in influencing deposit behaviour in the pre-1973 period, which was characterized by relative price stability.

The period 1980–85 was a period of economic recession in which the TD/GDP ratio averaged 49.5 percent. This was followed by a rapid

Table 10.3
Percent Composition of Financial Savings (Selected Years)

Institution	1990	1992	1994	1996	1998
Central Bank	9.3	8.3	10.4	10.4	9.3
Commercial banks	61.7	59.9	61.0	75.0	76.4
Life insurance company reserves	13.6	14.8	14.4	–	–
Credit union deposits	0.6	0.7	0.8	1.0	1.4
Share capital of credit unions	3.6	4.0	3.2	3.4	4.2
Trust and mortgage companies	10.8	11.0	9.2	8.8	6.6
Finance companies and merchant banks	1.4	1.3	1.0	1.4	2.1
Total	100.0	100.0	100.0	100.0	100.0

Source: Central Bank of Barbados, *Annual Statistical Digest* (1999).

growth of deposits in the late 1990s, stemming from economic expansion. By the year 2000, the banking system was inundated with liquidity, leading to an average financial deepening ratio of 91.8 percent between 1995 and 2000.

We also looked at the composition of financial savings during the 1990s. Table 10.3 shows that by 1998 commercial bank deposits were 76.4 percent of total financial savings. Credit union deposits and deposits of finance companies remained relatively small. Table 10.3 does not contain contractual savings such as premiums in life insurance companies and National Insurance contributions. Premium income in life insurance companies rose from $68.7 million in 1990 to $80.5 million in 1995. National Insurance contributions also increased from $133.9 million in 1990 to $250.7 million in 1998 (see Central Bank of Barbados, *Annual Statistical Digest*, 1999).

SOCIAL EFFICIENCY OF BANK LENDING

An important area of inquiry is the manner in which banks have allocated funds to various sectors of the economy. McClean (1975) and Thomas (1965) influenced my discussion of this issue. These works contain a similar thesis relating to lending in the colonial period and provide a useful frame of reference. McClean contends that the banks were "socially inefficient" because their lending policies were not consonant with the development goals of the economy. This was due to the banks' tendency to extend loans and advances with short maturities and their heavy emphasis on loans to the distribution sector. These tendencies were reinforced by strict creditworthiness criteria based on the borrower's character capability and the quality of collateral.

Thomas's argument proceeded from the view that the efficiency of any given pattern of loan distribution depends on an assessment of the credit needs of the economy. He argued that the banking system should attach less importance to financing the dependent ("generating") factors of the economy and more importance to financing production geared to the domestic market. Implicit in the normative arguments of both McClean and Thomas is the notion that bank credit should be "supply leading", in the sense that the banks should have attempted to promote investment behaviour outside the traditional sugar and import sectors. The Thomas/McClean thesis emphasized credit worthiness as a fundamental determinant of the loan supply function and the sectoral distribution of credit. A logical inference of their position is that the strict eligibility criteria in the colonial period reduced effective loan demand, thereby leading to surplus funds, which banks diverted to their head offices.

There is some validity to the contention that credit worthiness was perhaps the main determinant of loan supply in the colonial period. However, we question the plausibility of other views expressed by Thomas. Conceptually, Thomas's distinction between "dependent "and "independent" sectors is not particularly useful for analysing allocative or social efficiency. During the colonial period the credit needs of the dependent sugar and distribution sectors were understandably large relative to other sectors. In this period one should expect bank credit to fluctuate seasonally with movements in the sugar sector, which created lending opportunities in the overall trade sector. To argue that such lending was socially inefficient is to deny that the standard of living of the colony's population was intimately related to the fortunes of the sugar industry at that time. It is also arguable that the demand for domestic credit in incentive-aided firms, which relied on foreign capital, was not sufficiently strong to guarantee a noticeable shift in the banks' lending preferences during the 1950s and early 1960s.

I advance the position that even though strict credit-worthiness criteria remained important after 1970, the lending patterns of certain banks in Barbados began to reflect the increases in effective demand for working capital. However, before we deal with the working capital argument, it is necessary to touch on the measure of competition in the banking sector during the late 1960s, which helped to alter lending behaviour.

During the colonial period the banking system was strongly oligopolistic, that is, a few banks controlled credit allocation and deposit mobilization. Oligopolistic behaviour was reflected in a high degree of interest rate uniformity and limited access to credit by the non-bank public. In the late 1960s and early 1970s two banks with a British colonial tradition still maintained their strict eligibility criteria, emphasizing liquidity and safety in their operations. They continued to seek their security for loans mostly in terms of the quality of collateral. These banks recorded very few loan losses by relying on their prime established borrowers in the trading sector of the economy.

The American banks, which entered the credit market after 1968, did not show the same strict adherence to the commercial loan theory. Unlike banks with a British colonial tradition, they were unable to command a large number of established customers and were therefore prepared to take greater lending risks. These banks recorded higher levels of losses in sectors such as real estate, tourism and industry, which underwent an economic downturn between 1973 and 1975 (see Howard 1980). Our analysis should not be interpreted to mean that the banking system ceased to be oligopolistic because of the measure of competition introduced by the American banks. Their market share remained relatively small but their presence created the impetus for loan expansion and loan diversification by the aggregate banking system.

My examination of social efficiency requires an investigation into the maturity structure of bank credit. This is necessary for a critical evaluation of McClean's proposition that short-term credit was an indicator of social inefficiency. Banks concentrated on fulfilling the working capital requirements of their credit-worthy borrowers in the period after 1973. The years 1973–75 were characterized by recession and high inflation rates averaging 26 percent. Table 10.4 reveals that short-term lending was particularly high during these years, therefore showing a gradual decline. The Central Bank identified the inflation factor as a prominent cause of increased working capital requirements in construction, distribution and housing (Central Bank of Barbados, *Annual Report*, 1973:9, 1974:6). Much of this

Table 10.4
Maturity Structure of Commercial Bank Credit
(Period Averages)

Period	Short-Term Loans as % of Total Loans
1967–69	74.0
1970–74	72.2
1975–79	70.0
1980–85	63.2
1990–98	44.0

Note: Before 1961 short-term loans were classified as loans with original maturities of two years or less. From 1967 onwards, loans with original maturities three years or less were short-term loans, including overdrafts.

Source: Central Bank of Barbados, *Annual Statistical Digests* (1979, 1987, 2002).

credit was in the form of overdrafts and bridging loans. At the same time a few banks reported that some small exporters had become "bad credit risks" as a result of a sharp decline in external demand for manufactured goods. These factors reinforced the banks' tendency to lend short in a period when real interest rates were strongly negative.

The predominance of short-term lending was also attributable to other institutional features of the Barbadian financial system. Worrell and Prescod's (1983) view that there is probably no measurable shortage of venture capital except for first-time exporters and small businesses seems plausible. They argue that local investment is mainly undertaken by conglomerates and large firms with the capacity for internal finance and for switching funds between sectors. Additionally, much of the investment in fixed capital is financed by government or from abroad. Worrell and Prescod's argument is supported by the fact that foreign capital constitutes over 30 percent of capital formation. In this system, therefore, it is conceivable that the demand for long-term credit was to a large extent accommodated outside the commercial bank system.

The foregoing analysis constitutes a reassessment of McClean's contention that short-term credit, per se, is a measure of social inefficiency. We are inclined to the view of Khatkhate and Riechel (1980) that the "responsiveness" of banks to the specific requirements of the real sectors constituted a measure of efficiency. The essential need of the real sectors during recessionary periods was working capital. Further, such lending helped to cushion the immediate impact of exogenous price changes and may have been an important stabilization element.

The sectoral distribution of credit reflects the fact that during the late 1970s the Barbadian economy had become a service economy. Table 10.5 shows that during the 1970s the largest shares of credit went to the distribution sector, as well as the household (personal) and tourism sectors. Of course, expansion in tourism influenced distributive activities and construction. The proportion of credit to manufacturing was relatively higher during the 1980s. It is also evident that the shares of credit going to agriculture and distribution have declined since 1968. Let us first look at the reason for the decline in bank credit to agriculture.

The diminution in agriculture's share of credit is related to decision variables affecting the banks' loan supply function, as well as the deterioration in the performance of agriculture during the transition. First, on the supply side banks identified a higher level of risks in lending to non-sugar agriculture. These risks resulted from the perishable nature of food crops, marketing problems and the higher administrative costs of servicing small peasant loans. Although the banks advanced these reasons for the low level of lending to agriculture, one can also argue that food crop production follows a pronounced seasonal pattern and it is possible for banks to calculate, with some accuracy, the risks involved in cultivation.

Table 10.5
Sectoral Distribution of Commercial Bank Credit (Percent)

Sector	1970	1974	1980	1984	1990	1997
Agriculture	6.7	7.5	3.6	5.9	2.4	2.3
Manufacturing	7.1	9.8	17.3	15.3	14.0	5.5
Distribution	17.0	20.2	16.0	14.3	16.5	13.1
Tourism	13.0	10.0	11.4	12.9	6.8	9.8
Public utilities	9.4	2.8	5.6	7.4	1.8	1.3
Construction	9.2	12.9	7.2	4.4	4.0	4.6
Personal	18.5	23.2	24.6	19.9	22.9	37.1
Services	3.5	9.2	5.9	6.2	17.2	12.7
All other	15.6	4.4	8.4	13.7	14.4	13.6
Total	100.0	100.0	100.0	100.0	100.0	100.0

Source: Central Bank of Barbados, *Annual Statistical Digest* (1981, 1987, 1999).

A more important reason is that the banks do not see small farmers as sufficiently credit worthy in terms of their ability to offer the type of collateral security sought by the banks. This is so in areas where farmers do not own land but are involved in livestock production. On the demand side, the slow progress toward increasing agriculture's share of credit is related to the decline in that sector's role in economic activity.

Additionally, there was an institutional shift in lending to the sugar industry after the Central Bank started operations in 1973. The Central Bank provided rediscounts directly to the Sugar Industry Agricultural Bank (SIAB) to finance sugar operations. This was a more efficient route for injecting funds into the sugar industry. As a result, the demands on commercial banks by planters for sugar financing were reduced commensurately. The rediscount facility eased pressure on commercial banks' having to manage wide swings in their liquidity requirements (Howard and Wapensky, 1974).

The manufacturing sector has never been a prime target for commercial bank credit. Small export manufacturers, especially those originating in the 1970s, are at a disadvantage in acquiring credit. The group compares unfavourably with "enclave" manufacturers, as well as traditional large-scale manufacturers of margarine, soap and edible oil. This last group, which was prominent during the 1950s, has maintained close economic and financial links with the distribution sector.

The pattern of credit distribution changed in the 1990s as banks extended an increased proportion of credit to the personal and service sectors. This reflected the fact that Barbados had become a service economy where over 70 percent of the country's GDP was derived from services. Table 10.5 shows that in 1997, the major sectors using credit were distribution, the personal or household sector and the service sector, which includes transport, professional services and other governmental services. The decline of the manufacturing sector is reflected in the small 5.5 percent of loans going to that sector in 1997. The same is true for the agricultural sector, where sugar has declined since the 1960s.

Our analysis also shows that short-term lending averaged 44 percent for the period 1990–98 (see Table 10.4). Close inspection of the data leads to the view that there was a shift to longer-term credit in the late 1990s, and the sectors receiving increases in such credit were the tourism and household sectors. This supports our view that in order to satisfy the long-term demands of the service economy, the banks have increased their long-term lending, which contrasts with the predominance of short-term credit in the early post-colonial economy.

FINANCIAL INNOVATION

Financial innovation was a characteristic of the Barbadian financial structure in the late 1980s and 1990s. Government played an important role in providing tax incentives to stimulate the growth of the capital market, and to encourage international banking. Fabozzi et al. (1994:24) have identified a number of causes of financial innovation. These include changes in computer and telecommunications technologies, greater sophistication and training among professional market participants, competition among financial intermediaries, incentives to circumvent regulations and tax laws, and changing global patterns of financial wealth. Innovation in the Barbadian context has been designed to provide alternative avenues for investment, as well as to achieve benefits from the globalization of financial flows.

The first major innovation was the introduction of the Securities Exchange of Barbados (SEB) in 1987. The rationale for the SEB is to enhance capital market development. Most firms in Barbados rely on bank loans rather than equity for financing investment. Craigwell and Grandbois (1999) have maintained that equity investment has become necessary to absorb the excess liquidity in the financial system.

The SEB is a small financial institution compared with stock markets in developed countries. The number of firms trading on the SEB was twenty in 1999. The SEB is not price efficient in the informational sense defined by Fama (1970). A price-efficient market is one in which security prices reflect all available information. Craigwell and Grandbois (1999) have found that the SEB is financially inefficient.

Another innovation that started before 1990 is offshore banking. Doyle and Johnson (1999) estimated that Barbados had forty-four licensed offshore banks and five of these accounted for approximately 85 percent of the industry. They further estimated that the local expenditure by offshore banks was $50 million in 1996. Offshore banks employed 169 individuals in 1998, 77 percent of whom were local individuals. Doyle and Johnson reported that offshore banks contributed $1,771.5 million to the GDP of Barbados in 1998. However, offshore banking output is not normally included in the official GDP estimates of Barbados. Doyle and Johnson's GDP estimate for offshore banks cannot be regarded as conclusive, because the methodology for calculating offshore output needs to be defined more clearly.

Another significant financial innovation is the institution of mutual funds. These constitute a pool of savings contributed by many investors, and used to purchase a portfolio of securities. The mutual fund sells shares to the public and reinvests those shares in a portfolio of securities. Mutual funds help to diversify savings and minimize financial risk. They also provide investors with liquidity because the shares are redeemable. A mutual fund also provides professional management of investors' funds. In Barbados the government has encouraged investment in mutual funds by allowing an income tax deduction of up to $10,000 from assessable income.

There were three mutual funds in Barbados by the end of the year 2000, and they specialize in different types of instruments. For example, the Mutual Global Balanced Fund offers a mixture of investments, including equities, income and money market securities. In contrast to the balanced fund the Barbados National Bank offers separate mutual funds, including an income fund, a capital growth fund, a gift trust fund and a property and unlisted securities fund. The objective of the income fund is to provide high income by investing generally in government securities and high yielding stocks. The capital growth fund aims at long-term capital appreciation by investing in equities issued by companies. The property and unlisted fund is aimed at long-term capital appreciation through investment in real estate. The other mutual fund in Barbados is Fortress Mutual Fund.

The net assets of the mutual funds in 1999 were as follows: Mutual Global Balanced Fund $41 million and Fortress Mutual Fund $33.1 million. The performance of these funds was affected by the volatility of Caribbean stock markets. The international equity funds performed better because it was possible to hedge more effectively in international markets.

Venture capital funding is another innovation but the high-risk nature of this activity is a deterrent to many investors. Venture capital requires an adequate pool of risk capital and the availability of high performance projects. Venture capital investment in Barbados is small and was estimated at $23 million in 1998 (see the *Business Authority*, 18 October 1999, published by the *Barbados Advocate*).

The two venture capital companies during the 1990s were the Barbados Investment Fund (BIF) and the Enterprise Growth Fund (EGF). In 1992 the Central Bank of Barbados and the Caribbean Financial Service

Corporation (CFSC) established the BIF. The BIF was initially capitalized at $6.1 million, of which $5 million were contributed by the Central Bank and $1 million by CFSC, which is a funds manager. At the end of 1999 the BIF had invested $8 million in twenty-four projects. The EGF had also committed $2 million in venture capital to six Barbadian companies by the end of 1998 (*Business Authority*, 18 October 1999).

The Barbados government also introduced a range of medium-term investment instruments. These included savings bonds and national development bonds that were tax free up to a limit of $50,000. After 1987, refunds of income tax could be obtained in the form of interest-bearing tax refund certificates. Treasury notes are medium-term instruments with maturities of more than one year and up to ten years.

Zepherin and Seerattan (1997) also mentioned other financial innovations, such as automatic teller machines (ATM), credit and debit cards, sale and lease back arrangements and syndicated loans. It was, however, difficult to document the impact of these innovations.

CONCLUSION

The most significant feature of the Barbadian financial system is the dominant role played by commercial banks. The banks have increased considerably their share of assets and deposits in the financial system. The pattern of lending by commercial banks is now more socially efficient than in the past. The Barbadian financial system also experienced a significant degree of financial innovation. During the period studied the Central Bank introduced a measure of regulation into the financial system, thereby influencing savings mobilization, the expansion of credit and the overall financial climate.

11

C H A P T E R

Public Finance

INTRODUCTION

This chapter discusses the role of public finance in the development process. The analysis utilizes the distinction between the colonial development period (1946–60), the service economy period (1960–91), and the period of crisis and structural adjustment (1991–2000). In the specific context of public finance, certain colonial budgetary, legislative and tax norms continued into the 1960s. After Barbados gained independence from Britain in 1966, there was a transitional period (1965–73) when the government moved away from its reliance on cash reserves to greater dependence on the domestic financial system as a source of accommodation. The data and analysis in this chapter are derived from previous work by Howard (1979a, 1992, 2001b).

The genesis of public finance in the colonial development period can be interpreted within the context of structural dependence and sugar monoculture. The high level of structural dependence retarded the emergence of a public policy to diversify the productive base. Government relied heavily on revenue from sugar exports to maintain the growth of incomes and tax revenues. The level of sugar earnings also constrained the upward movement in current expenditure. The fiscal authorities found it relatively easy to raise revenues from indirect taxation, particularly customs duties. This was so because of the colony's heavy reliance on imports and the associated distributive activity.

In the service economy period, structural dependence was modified with the expansion of the foreign investment strategy, which imposed a constraint on the growth of tax revenues because of the liberal policy of tax incentives. This seeming contradiction, following an increased flow of capital into the economy, can be described as the "revenue deprivation effect" of foreign investment. However, public policy during this period placed more emphasis on growth with redistribution by providing a higher level of public goods. Howard (2002) has shown that the increase in public expenditure on public goods was in keeping with Wagner's law, which states that the share of the public sector in the economy increases with economic growth. Additionally, the period after 1973 saw greater flexibility in budgetary management by government's use of the Central

Bank as an instrument of deficit financing. In contrast to the period of colonial development, deficit financing by money creation had an expansionary effect on the monetary base as well as negative implications for the small country's balance of payments.

The period of crisis and structural adjustment is characterized by efforts to reduce the size of government, tax reform and privatization. The conceptual framework for understanding this period is globalization and neoliberalism, alluded to in Chapter 1.

COLONIAL BUDGETING

Government saving (the current account surplus) assumes greater significance as an instrument for financing capital expenditure when the public sector is unable to use deficit financing on a large scale. In the colonial period, the absence of a Central Bank as well as the inadequacy of the financial market led to heavy reliance on current surpluses. The budgetary system was designed to conserve reserves in times of a boom in sugar exports in order to spend them in times of slump. The accumulation of cash reserves was related to constraints imposed by the colonial monetary system. The colonial government had no control over the money supply, commercial bank credit or the structure of interest rates. This lack of monetary control meant that the government's power to pursue deficit financing was limited by the reserves at its disposal. Government spending was held in check by the level of sterling balances held by the colony.

Colonial budgetary policy enabled the public sector to accumulate sizeable reserve balances. These reserves were placed in three funds. The earmarked reserves were reserves set aside for specific purposes, for example, the Labour Welfare Fund. The Revenue Equalisation Fund was composed of payments from the surplus on the current and capital accounts to meet any marked fall in revenue and to enable the colonial government to avoid any reduction of the public service in bad years. The General Revenue Balance represented the colony's accumulated surplus after the annual transfers were made in respect of capital expenditure and the Revenue Equalisation Fund. Government's total reserve balance rose from $7.8 million in 1947 to $32.8 million in 1965. These reserves were held in cash, loans, local securities and investments in the Commonwealth. Prior to 1960, almost 70 percent of the reserves were held in cash, representing an uneconomical use of funds. After 1960, the colonial government shifted its reserves portfolio increasingly to securities and by 1965, 83 percent of the reserves were held in advances and securities.

The balanced budget philosophy of the colonial government was functional but anti-developmental. It was functional because balance-of-payments deficits were nonexistent in the small economy, and inflation was contained because of the constraint on spending. Balanced budgeting was anti-developmental because it rested too heavily on the cyclical movements of a single crop, and therefore straitjacketed the economy into operating in a low-level equilibrium trap. Although the colonial government recorded some success in the area of infrastructural spending, we shall see that its record in the areas of capital spending on education, health and social security was much less forward looking.

TAXATION IN THE COLONIAL DEVELOPMENT PERIOD

The tax system in a developing country should be income elastic in character to meet the long-run growth of government expenditures. If the tax system is not flexible, the fiscal authorities may have to resort to persistent tax rate increases or borrowing on a large scale. My work is therefore devoted to measuring the flexibility of the tax system under colonial conditions. We shall be concerned with movements in the tax ratio T/Y, as well as the buoyancy of the tax system, which measures the total response of tax revenue (that is, without adjusting for discretionary changes) to changes in income. Second, we examine the built-in flexibility of the income tax system. Our analysis is designed to show the extent to which the colonial government was able to mobilize involuntary savings through the use of direct and indirect taxation.

Tax revenues during the colonial period were derived mainly from customs and excise duties and income taxes. For almost the entire period, customs and excise duties constituted over 50 percent of total tax revenue, but between 1946–49 and 1950–54 the ratio of customs and excise duties to total tax revenue fell from 61.3 percent to 53.8 percent. At the same time, income taxes as a proportion of tax revenue rose from 34.6 percent to 41.3 percent. The increase in the relative importance of customs and excise duties between fiscal years 1955 and 1964 is due primarily to the introduction of higher ad valorem duties.

The Income Tax Act of 1921 introduced the income tax in Barbados. Initially, the tax was levied annually but with the introduction of the Pay-As-You-Earn (PAYE) system in 1957 it was deducted from salaries and wages on a non-cumulative basis. The Income Tax Act was amended in 1953 to increase the rate of tax on companies from 37.5 percent to 40 percent, where it remained until the end of the period.

During the colonial period Barbados, partly as a result of its high degree of openness, had a high tax ratio compared to other Caribbean territories. Following Chelliah (1971:258) the tax ratio (T/Y) indicates the degree of control exercised by the government over the disposition of purchasing power in the economy. A comparative analysis of four Commonwealth Caribbean territories done by David (1970) shows that in 1959 the tax ratio in Barbados was 18.7 percent compared to 20.05 percent for Guyana; 12.62 percent for Jamaica and 13.43 percent for Trinidad and

Tobago. By 1964, Barbados's tax ratio rose to 23.1 percent compared to 18.5 percent for Guyana; 17.3 percent for Jamaica and 13.5 percent for Trinidad and Tobago.

A more important measure of the sensitivity of taxes to income is the buoyancy coefficient calculated from the log linear equation:

$$\text{Log } T = \log a + b \log Y$$

where T is the total tax yield and B is the buoyancy coefficient. The buoyancy coefficient is calculated from a tax data series that is unadjusted for discretionary tax changes. Our reliance on the buoyancy coefficient is justified because of the low level of discretionary tax changes during the colonial period. A coefficient much higher than unity indicates that the tax system is highly responsive to income changes. For the total tax yield (T) the buoyancy coefficient was 1.046, slightly higher than unity, showing a tendency for total tax yield to vary proportionally with income. I advance the view later that the low built-in flexibility of the income tax may have reduced the overall buoyancy coefficients of the tax system. The buoyancy coefficients for income taxes and customs duties were 1.08 and 1.09, respectively, showing the same tendency to vary proportionally with income.

The size of the buoyancy coefficient can be explained by the tax structure, the incidence of tax evasion and the difficulty of administering the tax system. The developmental potential of the tax system may have been significantly reduced by institutional factors in the colonial period. For this reason I examined income tax flexibility, building on a previous study carried out by Bonnett (1975).

Bonnett's analysis utilized Pechman's (1956) measure of built-in flexibility, which rests on the concept of adjusted gross income (AGI). The latter forms the base on which deductions and personal exemptions are made and is defined as the aggregate of factor incomes accruing to households plus capital gains, minus transfer payments. Built-in flexibility is therefore defined as a relative change in tax liability divided by a change in AGI. Bonnett (1975) found that the built-in flexibility of the progressive income tax in Barbados between 1951 and 1962 was very low and sometimes negative. Our analysis examined the raw data relating to AGI, taxable income and tax liabilities for individuals, as well as some of the institutional reasons for low income tax yields.

One reason for the low built-in flexibility of income taxes in underdeveloped countries such as Barbados during this period was the difficulty of administering the tax. The system that existed prior to the PAYE system relied on individuals submitting a tax return form for each year and then paying the tax. As a result, there was a great discrepancy between AGI and the actual income recorded on tax returns. This phenomenon led to a low ratio of tax liabilities to AGI. We found that the ratio of taxable income to AGI averaged 24.5 percent between 1951 and 1962 while the average ratio of tax liabilities to AGI was a low 5.7 percent.

It is difficult to quantify the extent of tax evasion contributing to the low net tax yield. There were a large number of individuals in the zero tax rate bracket. However, these incomes may have been too small to significantly influence net tax yield. The introduction of the PAYE system in 1957 may have reduced somewhat the incidence of default, although loopholes continued to exist in the collection of taxes, especially from self-employed persons and MNCs, which may have been able to minimize corporation tax payments by means of transfer pricing. Also, there were difficulties of recording agricultural incomes in the peasant sector of the economy because many small farmers kept no records.

PUBLIC EXPENDITURE IN THE COLONIAL PERIOD

Let us examine the performance of public expenditure. Total current expenditure expanded immediately after World War II. This period was characterized by liberal grants from the British government under the Colonial Development Fund Act of 1929 and the Colonial Development and Welfare Acts of 1940 and 1945. In Barbados current expenditure grew from $6.6 million in 1946 to $9.6 million in 1950 to alleviate the hardships created by the war.

During the period 1950–53, budgetary policy, according to Beasley (1952), was framed on "caretaker" lines – restraining proposals for new items of revenue. After the period of rising commitments following the war, expenditure was restrained until it was ascertainable whether the cost of the full commitments for existing services, as well as increased costs of materials, could be adequately covered by revenue.

The period 1953–64 was an era of rapid growth, where capital expenditure grew at a compounded annual rate of 15.8 percent and current expenditure at a rate of 9.1 percent. This period was characterized by a deepening of the economic infrastructure as well as rapid expansion in the cost of maintaining the colonial administration. Toward the end of the period new initiatives were taken in the areas of housing, education, road building and the provision of social amenities during the transition to political independence in 1966.

Further analysis reveals that the category "general services" (which represents administrative spending) had the highest growth rate (13 percent) in the current account budget. High administrative costs were due to small size, which caused an absence of economies of scale in administration. Although small size may have undoubtedly increased administrative costs, its effect is difficult to quantify. High administrative costs were also due to the colonial type of administration. Colonial societies tended to have "top heavy" administrations with metropolitan officials paralleling and supervising the operations of local administrators.

Education and other social services (including health) recorded growth rates of 9.7 percent and 9.8 percent, respectively, on the current budget and 0.8 percent and 1.6 percent, respectively, on the capital budget. Although Barbados had a well-developed system of primary education, secondary education during the colonial period was regarded as a privilege set aside for the elite, and this partly explains the low level of capital expenditure on education during 1953–64. Most secondary schools, as well as primary schools, suffered from an acute problem of lack of accommodation. Moreover, the class-ordered educational system prevented the emergence of a fiscal policy geared to maximize employment in the colonial economy. Health services were not properly organized and the framing of health policy was difficult. There was no provision under the Public Health Act of 1908 for modern advances in public health and medical administration. However, plans for the building of a new hospital were conceived during the period.

Expenditure on economic services (which included transport and communications, agriculture, labour, public works and other miscellaneous services) had the lowest growth rate, of 5.9 percent on the current budget and 15.7 percent on the capital budget. The high level of capital spending on economic services was reflected in the *Five Year Plan of Development and Taxation* for Barbados (1952/53–1956/57), and the *Barbados Development Plan* 1955–60. These plans recognized the need for the building of a deep-water harbour, the development of water sources and road building projects. The Deep Water Harbour project, the most important achievement of the colonial administration, absorbed a large proportion of capital expenditure during these years. Despite this emphasis on infrastructure, the colonial government had not formulated a concept of development geared to reduce dualism by creating linkages between industry and agriculture. Development was confused with economic growth and the welfare implications of fiscal expenditures were not fully perceived. This is the basic weakness of colonial fiscal policy.

We can look briefly at the impact of the financing of capital expenditure on the public debt. Debt service in the colonial period was never a serious problem because the colonial monetary system was a constraint on assuming a debt that could not be sustained from revenues and foreign exchange receipts. The public debt of the colony comprised loans raised by the government by way of debenture issues under the Public Loan Act 1914-1 and the General Local Loan Act 1933-7. The government was also empowered to raise money by issuing debentures in the United Kingdom through the crown agents. Permission was also given to the government to borrow from the Revenue Equalisation Fund, pending the availability of money to be raised under the various loan acts.

The available data for the entire period do not permit a classification of the public debt into internal and external debt. The gross internal debt was 85.7 percent of total debt in 1955, but by 1965 this ratio fell to 40.5 percent. By contrast, the gross external debt rose from 14.3 percent of total debt in 1955 to 59.5 percent in 1965. The sharp rise in the external debt was due primarily to the Deep Water Harbour project, financed primarily by loans raised in the United Kingdom. For instance, at the end of the year 1965, $18 million (39 percent) of the debt was raised to finance this project. The borrowing at the start of the project is reflected in the sharp rise in the gross external debt from $0.7 million in 1958 to $13.1 million in 1959. Additionally, the rapid expansion of the public debt was due to direct public capital expenditure on the airport, housing, public buildings, roads and other projects.

BUDGETARY POLICY IN THE EARLY SERVICE ECONOMY PERIOD

The budgetary policy of the government evolved slowly after Independence. The early post-colonial approach to public sector financing was still influenced by the policy of generating revenue surpluses in the absence of a central bank. According to the *Barbados Development Plan* 1965–68, the budgetary policy of the government was guided by three normative principles. First, the yield of taxation should be sufficient to cover recurrent expenditure and also make a contribution to financing capital expenditure. Second, the tax burden should be equitably distributed. Third, taxation policy should contribute to economic growth. The emphasis on current account surpluses was reiterated in the *Development Plans* of 1969–72 and 1973–77 as well as in the annual budgets prior to 1973. Deficit financing became highly important after 1973 when the Central Bank began its operations.

It is important to state that a major departure from colonial budgetary policy was the post-independence emphasis on income redistribution. Colonial public policy was concerned more with economic growth as it related to sugar output than with the welfare effects of direct income redistribution strategies. In keeping with the dominant philosophy of that period, it was hoped that the fruits of export-propelled growth would somehow "trickle down" to the masses. The income redistribution strategy of the 1960s was not conceived in terms of fundamental tax reform but in terms of resource allocation policies that guaranteed a higher level of "social overheads". The post-colonial government adopted as an objective the provision of social goods such as health, education and low cost housing by increasing the aggregate tax burden. Howard (1992:45–53) provides a detailed analysis of public expenditure and comparisons with Jamaica and Trinidad and Tobago. In terms of direct income redistribution new emphasis was placed on social security through the instrument of payroll taxes (see Howard 1992:104–105). The Barbadian economy may have experienced some degree of redistribution during this period.

After 1977, the pattern of budgetary policy shifted to direct income redistribution through the budget. "Incremental redistribution" was attempted by the modification of income tax brackets and the provision of rebates for lower-income groups. Even though the government was still conscious of the need to generate a surplus on current account to reduce the balance-of-payments effect of Central Bank money creation, the budget after 1977 can be regarded more as an instrument of planning than an exercise in simply financing a current account deficit.

TAXATION IN THE SERVICE ECONOMY PERIOD
(UP TO 1979)

The period 1965–85 was characterized by an expansion of the tax ratio as well as policy-induced shifts in the structure of taxation. The ratio of total tax revenue to GDP rose from 22.4 percent in the period 1965–69 to 27.8 percent in the period 1975–79. This was due primarily to the growth of personal income taxation. The contribution of personal income taxation to total tax revenue rose from 20.5 percent in the period 1965–69 to 28.7 percent in 1975–79. On the other hand, indirect taxation fell sharply, from 55.4 percent of total tax revenue to 43.9 percent during the same period.

Direct taxation increased its relative importance in the service economy period as a result of the expansion in the tax base and administrative tax exchanges. This period was marked by the transfer of two local government taxes – the trade tax and the land tax – to central government revenues. The trade tax during the colonial period was based on the profits of people carrying on trade. When local government was abolished in 1967 the trade tax became part of the income tax. The trade tax, which was levied at 12 percent of profits in the colonial period, was raised to 20 percent in 1974 and constituted about 7 percent of income and profit tax revenue of the central government. This tax was abolished in 1977. The land tax in the colonial period was levied at different rates according to the parish in which it was levied. This tax also augmented the central government's direct tax revenue (Howard 1979a).

Indirect taxation fell as a ratio of tax revenue between 1965 and 1979 despite frequent discretionary changes in indirect tax rates and bases. For example, in 1974 a 5 percent sales tax was introduced with an estimated annual yield of $8 million. The switch to the Common External Tariff in 1973 led to the introduction of a wide range of import and consumption duties. Most budgets after 1967 introduced miscellaneous taxes and levies on commodities. The poor performance of indirect taxation between 1965 and 1979 is explained by the low elasticity and buoyancy of indirect taxation.

First, we look at the elasticity coefficient, drawing on work carried out by Holder (1982) for Barbados. Holder calculated tax elasticities, using a revenue series that was adjusted for discretionary tax changes between 1962 and 1980. His results showed that total tax revenue was quite inelastic between 1962 and 1980. The overall tax elasticity was 0.373, considerably less than unity. However, taxes on income and profit had an elasticity of 1.175, and total direct taxation an elasticity of 1.001. The elasticities for all other indirect taxes were much less than unity. The higher elasticities for income taxation partly explain the shift in the tax structure from indirect to direct taxes between 1965 and 1979.

The argument is advanced here that the inelasticity of indirect taxation is partly explained by the "revenue deprivation effect" of the foreign investment strategy. This effect expanded with the growth of the economy and inflation. Most import duties were on an ad valorem basis but government, through its tax incentive policy, was unable to realize increased revenue yield. Government therefore resorted to constant increases in other indirect tax rates outside the orbit of the Puerto Rican model. In addition, the rapidly expanded role of government in the construction industry after 1965 reduced the sensitivity of indirect taxation because imported materials designed for government projects were normally exempt from duty.

Second, I examined the buoyancy of direct and indirect taxation between 1965 and 1980. Regression results showed a buoyancy coefficient of 1.09 for total tax revenue, which does not differ significantly from the coefficient of 1.04 for the colonial period. This coefficient shows a tendency for total tax revenues to vary proportionally with income. Income taxes and total direct taxes had a buoyancy coefficient of 1.20, slightly higher than unity and also higher than the coefficient of 1.08 for the colonial period. The analysis reveals that direct taxation has been much more responsive to income changes during the course of development. The buoyancy coefficients for import duties and overall indirect taxes are slightly lower than unity. Import duties registered a coefficient of 0.8 and taxation 0.9. Low tax buoyancies may be due to a number of factors, including tax evasion, transfer pricing by multinational firms, lags in tax collection and structural problems in the economy. For an alternative analysis of tax buoyancy in Barbados, the reader is referred to Williams (2001).

Skeete, Coppin and Boamah (2003) used more advanced econometric techniques to estimate tax elasticities and tax buoyancies for the period 1977–99. Their results utilized cointegration analysis and were based on a long-run model and an error correction model. Indirect taxes were unresponsive in the long run, with an elasticity of 0.70, whereas the short-run elasticity was 1.14. The long-run indirect tax buoyancy was 1.54, while the short-run buoyancy was 1.22. Direct taxes showed long-run and short-run elasticities of 1.49 and 0.89, respectively. The buoyancies for direct taxes were 1.32 in the long run and 1.05 in the short run. The results show the importance of frequent discretionary changes in raising the tax buoyancies.

TAX REFORM (1977–86)

Taxation reform is an aspect of structural adjustment. Howard (1992) discusses the major principles of tax reform. These include equity, efficiency, simplicity, base broadening and cost effectiveness. In Barbados the equity principle guided the reforms before 1986, and was in keeping with the early post-colonial budgetary policy of income redistribution to the lower-income groups. Very little emphasis was placed on efficiency before 1986.

The principal factors influencing income tax reform between 1977 and 1986 were initially the inflationary impact of the oil crisis of 1973 and a conscious policy by the state to build a service economy by reducing the incidence of personal income tax. Between 1973 and 1977, there was no significant reform of the income tax system. During this period, government was concerned primarily with contractionary stabilization policy to curb consumption expenditure and correct the balance of payments. It was only after 1977 that income redistribution, by way of income tax reform, was regarded as a fundamental aspect of the government's budgetary policy.

The most important reform in the income tax system prior to 1986 was the introduction of a tax credit system in 1977. The primary purpose of the tax credit system was to reduce or remove completely the incidence of income tax for the lowest-income groups. For example, a taxpayer with income of $6,000 per year or less, whose net tax due was less than $60 in 1976, was not required to pay income tax. The tax credit system was abolished in 1986. This analysis is based on Howard (1987).

Other reforms in the income tax system between 1977 and 1986 can be described as gradualist in nature. Slight adjustments were made to the top rate of income tax, and the income tax bands were widened to accommodate wage changes. In fiscal 1979–80, a maximum marginal rate of 70 percent was charged on incomes over $30,000. The bands were widened in fiscal 1980–81, but high marginal rates remained on incomes over $30,000.

An evaluation of the income tax reforms between 1977 and 1986 shows that middle- and upper-income groups did not benefit significantly from the tax adjustments. The tax credit system eased the burden for large numbers in the lower-income groups. It is estimated that the reforms of 1980–81 freed 29 percent of the labour force or 30,000 people at the bottom of the tax scale from the income tax net.

TAX REFORM (1986–97)

Barbados experienced three major tax reforms in 1986, 1992 and 1997. The most important features of the 1986 income tax reform were the introduction of a standard deduction of $15,000 and the abolition of income tax for individuals earning $15,000 or less (Howard 1992). This reform reduced tax payable for the entire set of taxpayers at a cost of almost $80 million over a two-year period. The 1986 tax reform can be considered a massive income tax cut, but it did not achieve many of the principles of tax reform indicated earlier. The 1992 income tax reform attempted to achieve efficiency and cost effectiveness. The third reform in 1997 was the introduction of the value added tax (VAT). This section looks only at income tax reform. The reader is referred to Howard (2001b:233–238) and Alleyne and Howard (2003:17–44) for an extensive analysis of the VAT in Barbados. Primarily because of the detailed nature of the VAT system, considerations of space do not allow us to give an adequate treatment of the VAT in this chapter. The fiscal system came to rely heavily on indirect taxes, and the VAT became the highest revenue-yielding tax instrument by the year 2000.

The old income tax system between 1986 and 1992 became highly complicated for two reasons. First, a complex system of itemized allowances and deductions emerged, enabling certain individuals to claim allowances well in excess of $15,000. These numerous tax breaks and shelters introduced an element of discrimination into the old tax system, which considerably reduced tax neutrality. Further, the types of itemized deductions were not related to the need for horizontal equity. High-income individuals were in a better position to take advantage of these opportunities, particularly the unlimited mortgage interest deduction, because lower-income individuals were less able to satisfy borrowing criteria. The 1986 reform therefore failed to simplify the tax system.

Second, the old income tax system became overburdened with levies in the form of payroll taxes. These levies were really surtaxes on income and were earmarked for specific purposes. The money value of levies, including the transport, health, training and employment levies was increased after 1986, in response to severe recession in the Barbadian economy. Additionally, an individual stabilization tax (or surtax) was imposed on incomes. This tax rose from 1.5 percent on assessable income below $15,000 to 4 percent on the part of income exceeding $15,000. The IMF mission to Barbados in 1992 reported that at income levels of $30,000, the effective rate of income tax, including PAYE, levies, national insurance contributions and stabilization tax, reached 55 percent of assessable income.

Mascoll (1991) found that the 1986 tax measures benefited mostly upper-income individuals who experienced a fall in their effective income tax rate from 28.3 percent in 1985 to 19.2 percent in 1987. The average effective tax rate for middle-income taxpayers fell from 12.9 percent in

1985 to 12.8 percent in 1987. For low-income taxpayers, the effective tax rate decreased from 9.6 percent in 1985 to 8.8 percent in 1987. The levies and stabilization tax mentioned above were particularly burdensome on middle- and low-income individuals.

The major features of the 1992 reforms were the reduction of the maximum marginal tax rate from 50 percent to 40 percent, the elimination of most itemized deductions, and the reduction of the standard deduction from $15,000 to $13,000. These reforms caused a decline in overall effective tax rates. It is estimated that total effective tax rates for persons earning $13,000 declined from 14 percent in 1992 to 10.9 percent in 1993. By 1994, total tax rates fell to 8.2 percent for the two lowest assessable income groups. The steepest decline in total effective tax rates were for the income group earning $100,000. The tax reforms, therefore, significantly benefited individuals in the upper-income group. See Howard (2001a) for a more detailed analysis of the overall impact of the tax reforms.

The 1992 tax reform in Barbados was part of the worldwide tax reform movement, as well as an essential component of the country's structural adjustment programme initiated in 1991. The principal goals of tax reform were to increase the efficiency, equity and simplicity of the tax system. Over the years, the Barbadian tax system had become unfair, highly complex and contained a large number of concessions and preferences that favoured the rich and propertied interests.

Under a programme of structural adjustment, a uniform tax system is best for resource allocation. A less discriminatory tax regime makes for simplicity and reduces political patronage in the form of tax shelters. A highly progressive system places pressure on government to discriminate by way of preferential treatment of high-income individuals. Highly progressive systems also encourage tax evasion.

The 1992 Barbadian tax reform embodied some of the modernist principles of the worldwide tax reform movement discussed in earlier sections. These are simplicity, efficiency, revenue maintenance, equity, cost effectiveness and base broadening.

The first feature of the 1992 reform was the simplification of the tax system. The elimination of stabilization taxes and various levies eased the burden on lower-income groups and improved the simplicity of administering the tax system. Simplicity was also achieved by the flat rate of 40 percent on incomes above $37,200 and the new standard deduction of $13,000.

Simplification meant the elimination of itemized deductions. Tax authorities were no longer required to scrutinize numerous documents submitted by taxpayers to support claims for deductions. Simplification also guaranteed the removal of incentives for tax avoidance by highly paid individuals, by reducing their ability to exploit loopholes in the tax code.

Tax systems with less progressivity favour efficiency. The 1992 tax reform, by lowering the top marginal rate, improved the system's ability to reduce the negative substitution effects of taxes on income, thereby promoting efficiency, that is, lowering the welfare loss associated with high marginal rates.

The 1992 reform was more revenue-efficient than the previous system. Revenue efficiency was achieved by broadening the tax base, the abolition of itemized deductions and the lower $13,000 standard deduction. Despite base broadening, a large section of the labour force continued to be exempt from PAYE taxation.

Was the 1992 reform cost-effective? Under the old system (1986–92), the cost of tax administration was high. There was the administrative costs of collecting about seven direct taxes (including levies), when two or three taxes would have served the same purpose because all revenues were placed in a single consolidated fund. Although we have found no estimates of the administrative costs of both systems, a less complex system should certainly be more cost-effective.

The 1992 reform broadened the tax base and, therefore, allowed fewer taxes and lower tax rates on a broader range of incomes. This improved efficiency. Tax systems that are highly discriminatory, like the 1986–92 system, channel resources into undesirable areas. Further, the broadening of the tax base to include pensions affected pensioners with income below $20,000. Only pensioners with above-average income received benefits from the exclusion of income under the old system. The previous exclusion of high-income pensioners placed a higher burden of tax on workers with dependents, than on high-income retired individuals.

THE FIRST STABILIZATION CRISIS 1981

The principal fiscal problem immediately after 1980 was the management of the government's budget deficit. The establishment of the Central Bank of Barbados brought with it the authority to create money and thus the ability to finance the government's budget deficit. Prior to 1981, the budget deficit was well managed and financed by domestic and foreign sources with the Central Bank contributing significantly in 1977. However, Central Bank money creation before 1981 did not cause a very serious problem for the balance of payments.

The year 1981 was a turning point in Barbadian fiscal management. In that year, the overall fiscal deficit of $181 million was financed by foreign borrowing and Central Bank money creation. This year was an election year in which the financing of an unusually heavy government capital works programme took place against a background of recessionary conditions in the world economy. The massive capital expenditure of

$173.1 million was an important contributor to a fall in international reserves of $40.9 million between December 1980 and December 1981.

Partly as a result of the expansionary monetary policies of 1981 and the deepening world recession of 1982, the Barbadian economy became locked into balance-of-payments difficulties which government stabilization policies were unable to solve. These policies were announced in two budgets: the so-called mini-budget of September 1981 and the annual budget of March 1982. The stabilization programmes emphasized measures designed to curb aggregate demand and reduce the negative pressure on the balance of payments. Particular stress was placed on wage and credit restraints in both the private and public sectors, cuts in capital expenditures and control over the growth of current expenditure. Other fiscal measures included transport and health levies and a range of indirect taxes.

In 1982, the government was concerned that the widening of the current account deficit on the balance of payments required the intervention of the IMF. The authorities maintained that the IMF was the cheapest source of finance for balance-of-payments support. The government also emphasized that the problems of the economy were due primarily to the world recession rather than to domestic monetary and fiscal policies.

Despite the defence by government of its management of the economy, it is a valid criticism that the intervention of the IMF in the Barbadian economy in late 1982 partly reflected the effects of the heavy capital spending of 1981 and the accompanying policy of Central Bank money creation. The IMF Standby Arrangement specified quantitative limits on Central Bank net domestic assets and the net credit of the banking system to the nonfinancial public sector. These policies were designed to restore fiscal and balance-of-payments equilibrium.

We must conclude that the emphasis on deficit financing in the late 1970s and 1980s represented a fundamental shift in fiscal management. The major lesson of 1981 is that governments in developing countries should not overuse central bank money creation in the pursuit of aggressive fiscal policies. Many central banks in these countries seem unable to resist the governments' request for credit within the context of the power relations and political realities attending the nature of the constitutional relationship between the two institutions.

THE SECOND STABILIZATION CRISIS 1990–91

The Barbadian stabilization experience is interesting because it is the story of a small economy that has successfully applied an IMF programme in restoring fiscal and balance-of-payments equilibrium. The Barbadian economy slumped into crisis in 1991, as a result of a sharp deterioration in the fiscal and balance-of-payments deficits. Howard (1992) reports that the fiscal deficit climbed to a record high of $244.0 million in 1990, and was heavily financed by the Central Bank. The foreign reserves fell by $100.0 million in 1990. The heavy deficit occurred just before the general elections of 1991 in the context of a decline of the real sector.

The stabilization programme in Barbados was designed to reduce the fiscal deficit and restore balance-of-payments equilibrium. The programme included an 8 percent cut in public sector wages and salaries, massive downsizing in the public sector, and indirect tax measures. A wages and incomes protocol was also implemented (see Downes 1994 and Haynes 1997). However, the Barbadian authorities led by Prime Minister Erskine Sandiford were able to resist the IMF's demands for a devaluation of the Barbadian dollar. The Barbadian authorities insisted on maintaining the pegged rate of exchange at whatever cost.

The stabilization programme was successful. The economy recorded growth of 5.2 percent in 1996 compared with a decline of 5.7 percent in 1992. The net international reserves improved substantially from $35.0 million in 1991 to $577.5 million in 1996. Current account surpluses and smaller government deficits were also recorded between 1992 and 1996. Inflation remained low and there was a recovery in the export sectors as well as investor confidence.

A number of lessons can be learnt from the Barbadian stabilization experience. I agree with Haynes (1997) that the Barbadian experience shows that a fixed exchange rate is sustainable, but it requires disciplined fiscal and monetary policies. Further, the government should not rely too heavily on the central bank to finance the fiscal deficit. This often leads to foreign reserves depletion. The Barbadian case also reveals that a successful incomes policy depends on cooperation between the government, private sector and trade unions.

PRIVATIZATION

Privatization was an important component of structural adjustment policies. Its primary objectives were to improve economic efficiency and reduce the size of government. Howard (1992) presents some of the theoretical arguments for privatization, which include improving the level of competitiveness, reducing the budget deficit and eliminating political interference in the day to day running of public enterprises. Privatization also broadens the capital market through increased share ownership among workers and firms.

Between 1986 and 1991, the Barbadian government adopted an ambivalent attitude toward divestment. The manifesto of the Democratic Labour Party (DLP) government, which assumed power in 1986, stated that the public sector must continue to play a role in the provision of private goods and services for purchase by individuals. It was the intention of the DLP government to invest in and promote the production and distribution of private goods, in areas where government initiative was required. The government's strategy had three major objectives:

1. To emphasize joint ventures between government and the private sector;
2. To put an end to the practice of allowing publicly owned businesses producing non-strategic goods to continue to incur losses;
3. To undertake complete divestment in cases where analysis reveals that such action is appropriate. (See the DLP's Manifesto, 1986:7.)

There is strong evidence to support the view that the DLP government was in favour of a plan to privatize the Hilton Hotel, the Heywoods Holiday Village Hotel, and the Arawak Cement Plant. Errol Barrow, the prime minister of Barbados at that time, articulated this position. His plan rested on the view that the taxpayers should be relieved of the burden of supporting these enterprises, since the tax money could be more effectively used for providing housing. Further, Barrow sanctioned the discontinuation of the government-owned Caribbean Airways in 1987, because the national airline was unprofitable.

Barrow's approach to divestment rested purely on the argument that it was necessary to reduce the high costs to the government of operating inefficient parastatals. However, it should be noted that the Barbados Transport Board, which operated with large annual deficits, was not on the government's agenda for divestment. Perhaps the government regarded the Transport Board as a strategic good in a social sense. Shortly before his death in 1987, Barrow decided against privatization of the Hilton and Heywoods Hotels and the Arawak Cement Plant. However, Heywoods Hotel was eventually privatized.

For the period between 1987 and 1990, I have not seen any documentary evidence to suggest that the Barbados government was firmly in favour of divestment of public sector enterprises. The IMF programme in Barbados in 1991 required the Barbados government to reduce its transfers to statutory corporations, and the government appeared to be under pressure from the IMF and the World Bank to privatize certain public enterprises. The IMF letter of intent of October 1991 acknowledged the government's intention of divesting certain private enterprises, including the Arawak Cement Plant, the Pine Hill Dairy, and Caricargo. However, the DLP government went out of power in 1994.

The Barbados Labour Party (BLP) government after 1994, under the leadership of Prime Minister Owen Arthur, was influenced by the neoliberal approach to privatization. The Barbados government privatized the Barbados National Bank (BNB) and the Insurance Corporation of Barbados (ICB) after 2000. These privatizations were part of the structural adjustment approach to make these operations more efficient and competitive.

PUBLIC SECTOR REFORM

Public sector reform is another aspect of the structural adjustment process in Barbados. The purpose of public sector reform is to modify the role of government and improve its efficiency in a market-oriented economy. The 1998 Barbados White Paper on Public Sector Reform outlined the government's intention to make Barbados more competitive internationally by enhancing productivity, optimizing the use of resources and improving the government's operating systems.

The approach to public sector reform was determined by a number of governmental organizational problems. These included a bureaucratic structure characterized by excessive red tape, long delays, over-centralization, and the inability of managers to delegate duties effectively. The bureaucracy was noted for its high operating costs, poor human resource management and inadequate training of staff. Financial systems lacked proper internal controls.

The reforms attempted to improve human resource management, financial management, the delivery of services and the legal aspects of government organizations. The human resource strategy emphasized upgrading the management information system, training of staff and the adoption of appropriate policies for acting appointments and the recruitment of staff. The establishment of an appropriate appraisal system would support this approach.

In the area of financial management there was need for greater accountability in the use of public funds. Thus the appropriate strategy for improving financial efficiency emphasized the acquisition of accurate financial information, transparency in financial transactions, better management of supplies and improved property management. The White Paper also noted that multi-year financial planning would be introduced to improve budgetary management.

The adoption of customer charters would improve the delivery of services. A customer charter is the pledge of the agency's intention to honour the standards and quality of performance. Such charters would also provide assurances that there would be no discrimination in the provision of services. However, in the year 2000 it was too early to assess the progress of public sector reform in Barbados. The process would take a large number of years to change an organizational culture that was more government oriented than customer oriented.

SUMMARY

I have traversed a broad field in public finance. The policy of government changed from colonial budgeting to deficit financing. More emphasis was placed on the use of public expenditure to provide essential public goods. Despite the careful management of the public finances for most years, the Barbadian government experienced two serious financial crises in 1981 and 1991 when the country applied to the IMF for balance-of-payments support. Privatization and public sector reform attempted to improve public sector performance. The precise impact of these strategies cannot be evaluated in this study since they started towards the end of our survey period.

12

Concluding Observations

THE MAJOR FINDINGS

This book has presented a historical/structural analysis of Barbadian economic development since World War II. A central argument developed in Chapter 2 is that Lewis's theoretical framework helps us to understand the rationale for the operational industrialization model adopted by Barbados. Chapter 2 also explained why it is necessary to employ a structuralist dependency perspective to identify the institutional factors that determined the dependent path of the economy. Our exposition alluded to some of the socio-political factors influencing resource allocation but the work emphasized mainly economic processes. The work also mentioned the influence of globalization and neoliberalism towards the end of the period.

The plantation, small size and openness were fundamental determinants of the nature of the transition. The growth of the plantation system and labour surplus under colonialism provided the institutional framework for the survival of sugar after World War II. Plantation capitalism was buttressed by the alliance between the mercantile and planter interests that ensured a continued pattern of trade with the metropole. The resurgence of the plantation system was aided by the necessary preoccupation of the political leaders with gradualist decolonization, as well as the emergence of a neomercantilist philosophy sanctioned by Moyne, Benham and Gallotti.

Small economic size reinforced the underdevelopment biases inherent in plantation production during the early post-war period. The size phenomenon partly explains why the Barbadian economy remained locked into a staple producer relationship with the metropole. Size alone, however, cannot explain the dynamic process of dependent structural change. I advanced the view in Chapter 3 that the policy of the Barbadian government was the primary determinant of structural change after 1960. The foreign investment strategy was the most important aspect of dependent capitalism. It was hoped that local entrepreneurship would thrive as a result of the impetus provided by the Puerto Rican strategy, but the economy was never able to generate its own internal dynamism or substantially reduce the labour surplus on the basis of the foreign investment strategy. Indeed, unemployment remained an intractable problem throughout the period we have studied.

A major finding of this work is that a significant degree of dependent structural change was achieved in the Barbadian economy. However, such change was disarticulated in the sense that no strong linkages were forged between the various sectors of the economy. This is explained by the export orientation of the primary sector and the import dependence of most industries. The export orientation of agriculture meant that there was very little effort to create a strong agro-industrial base. The dependent nature of structural change meant that the dynamic of each sector was determined predominantly by external market conditions.

Structural adjustment towards the end of the period attempted to improve economic efficiency. This was done by the implementation of policies for trade liberalization, tax reform, public sector reform, privatization and export promotion. Financial liberalization was not vigorously pursued. However, with the exception of tax reform it was difficult to determine empirically the precise impact of other structural adjustment policies before 2000.

A central theme of this study was the analysis of the extent of foreign capital in the Barbadian economy. We noticed that foreign capital took three principal forms: colonial aid, private settler-type foreign investment and foreign borrowing. Colonial aid was a manifestation of the British policy of responsible trusteeship. During the early post-war period colonial aid supplemented loans raised in the United Kingdom. The aid programme took the form of relatively small Colonial Development and Welfare (CD and W) grants, which totalled $3 million or 8.5 percent of actual capital expenditure between 1955 and 1960. These low levels of aid were predicated on the view held by the Colonial Office that each colony should fully utilize its own resources in the financing of its social services. Loan financing was used primarily in the building of the Deep Water Harbour.

Settler-type private foreign capital investment predominated the manufacturing and tourism sectors after 1960. The period of the 1970s revealed that the ratio of foreign investment to initial investment in manufacturing was usually over 50 percent, reaching a high of 91.4 percent in 1977. In tourism, settler-type foreign investment was highest in luxury class hotels while local investment was confined to smaller hotels. Although settler-type foreign investment had a positive impact on capital formation, the government was deprived of revenue through the operation of the tax incentive programme. There is, however, no firm evidence to show that foreign capital retarded the growth of total domestic savings or inhibited local entrepreneurship.

The political status of Barbados changed in 1966 when it achieved independence from Britain. This political factor largely explains why public sector foreign borrowing became more important in the context of development planning. Immediately after independence, government showed a reliance on international development agencies for financing. After 1970 market borrowing became highly important to finance large capital works programmes. The emergence of an aggressive public sector philosophy in the late 1970s was not tempered by the world recessionary conditions of 1980 and 1981. As a result, the government sought IMF assistance in 1982 because of the balance-of-payments problems associated with high levels of capital spending.

Dependent development was associated with the decline of the primary sector. This phenomenon was due not so much to the direct impact of the foreign investment strategy, but to specific economic and noneconomic factors affecting the sugar industry. The remarkable resurgence of the sugar industry in the 1950s came to an end in the late 1960s when the state pursued a land use policy that permitted subdivision of many plantations into two-acre lots and their subsequent sale. This policy caused the alienation of 12,175 acres of arable land from sugar cane production between 1966 and 1976, and had the undesirable effect of increasing land speculation. This policy is perhaps the most important factor leading to the steep fall in output in the late 1960s and early 1970s. The decline in the financial viability of the sugar industry is to be explained primarily, though not exclusively, by sharply rising production costs simultaneously with a declining volume of output.

Agricultural diversification was an instrument of structural adjustment. However, attempts to stimulate export crops other than sugar met with only moderate success, reinforcing the view that sugar is perhaps the best export crop suited to the Barbadian institutional environment. Cotton, for instance, encountered problems of labour shortage and insect pests. Onion exports were usually small. Despite these difficulties with export crops, Barbados became self-sufficient in vegetable production. This self-sufficiency provides reasonable ground to argue that food self-reliance, particularly in food crop production, is a feasible development option available to policy-makers. Such a policy may also generate a marketable surplus for export.

Our empirical analysis of the industrialization strategy highlighted some of the shortcomings of settler-type foreign investment. The analysis showed the heavy dependence of manufacturing on the domestic market. The exceptions were clothing and electronic components. We also noted the high initial costs of providing jobs and the tendency for capital intensity to expand in some industries during the 1980s. We attempted to support our analysis by examining indices such as value added per employee (V/L), and the share of wages in value added (WL/V). Although our results pointed to high levels of capital intensity in the chemical and beverage industries, some caution was advised in the interpretation of these indices.

This book also noted the limitations of the foreign investment strategy as a generator of employment, thereby supporting the previous early findings of Jefferson (1971) for Jamaica. The growth rate of employment tended to lag behind the growth rate of value added. Our interpretation of this fact rests on two explanations. First, the low growth rate of employment in manufacturing may be attributable to high levels of capital intensity, rising labour productivity or both. Second, the small size of the domestic market, particularly in the 1960s, limited the possibilities of import substitution and employment growth. The growth of manufacturing exports was slowed by the fall in external demand during the 1980s and 1990s, thereby constraining the expansion of employment.

Our examination of the findings on labour migration revealed that most of the migrants in the period of colonial development were highly unskilled. The proportion of skilled migrants rose after 1960, averaging around 33.7 percent by 1964. An examination of secondary data showed that skilled labour to the United States constituted about 8.6 percent of total migrants to that country between 1967 and 1976. Our study noted that most skilled labour went to the United Kingdom. Migration undoubtedly helped to relieve surplus labour on the land and to some extent contributed to foreign exchange earnings by way of remittances. However, migration was a palliative rather than a cure for the unemployment problem.

This study also made specific findings with respect to the behaviour of the import sector. Import substitution should lead to a high share of intermediate goods in total imports. It was found that the proportion of intermediate goods in total imports was well above 35 percent for most of the period between 1960 and 2000. Intermediate goods constituted the highest proportion of imports. At the same time the rise in the share of capital goods to total imports confirmed our theoretical expectations.

Another interesting finding was the degree of import substitution achieved in food output. Generally speaking, dependence on food imports remained high between 1960 and 2000. However, there was positive import substitution in vegetable production.

High levels of success were achieved in mobilizing both voluntary and involuntary savings. The savings mobilization ratio TD/GDP rose between 1950 and 2000. Our analysis in Chapter 10 indicated the dominance of the commercial banking system and the degree of financial innovation achieved in the Barbadian economy.

Our findings on financial resource allocation suggest that although credit worthiness remained an important variable in the loan supply function, the demand for working capital became a critical factor in the allocation of short-term credit during the 1970s. This was primarily because of the existence of inflation rates averaging 26 percent annually between 1973 and 1975. Another finding was that bank credit was more efficiently allocated between 1970 and 2000, as the banks sought to accommodate the growing needs of tourism, construction and public utilities. The only instance where credit was found to be inefficiently allocated was in the household sector. The level of spending in this sector was sustained as a result of high levels of foreign borrowing by the banking system, particularly in the 1970s.

Non-bank intermediaries played a smaller though important role in mobilizing financial savings in the Barbadian economy. The insurance companies were significant in mobilizing contractual savings. Most non-banks invested mainly in government treasury bills and debentures. Other financial instruments such as development bonds became important toward the end of the period. Our findings on the non-bank sector point to the need for policy-makers to increase the number of financial instruments and create incentives for the public to invest in securities.

The public sector was the major catalyst of dependent development. During the colonial period, the highly skewed distribution of income in the economy as well as administrative problems limited the extent to which the colonial government could raise revenues from income taxation. The latter lacked flexibility as a revenue-raising device. Indirect taxation sustained the upward movements in revenues before 1965. The development of the economy between 1965 and the late 1970s underlined the importance of the income tax as a revenue stabilization device. In large measure, inflation exerted a positive influence on the nominal value of income tax receipts. The buoyancy coefficient of income taxation was 1.2 between 1965 and 1980, slightly higher than the coefficient of 1.08 for the colonial period. Our findings also revealed that indirect taxation was quite insensitive to income changes for most of the period after 1965. We attributed this phenomenon largely to the revenue deprivation effect of the foreign investment strategy. It was found that this model, as well as the introduction of the Common External Tariff in 1973, led to a decline in the effective import tax rate (the ratio of import duties to imports) from 12.5 percent in 1963 to 7.8 percent in 1975. In the 1980s, consumption taxes and stamp duties were the principal instruments relied upon to recoup revenue lost from the fall in the import duty yield and income tax cuts. The tax reform of 1986 and 1992 improved the efficiency of the tax system.

Despite the increased efficiency of the public sector in mobilizing involuntary savings, deficit financing became increasingly important after 1970, partly as a result of inflation and partly because the high level of capital expenditure internalized large recurrent costs in the budget. The public sector became more reliant on Central Bank money creation as a source of accommodation. The financing of the government deficit by domestic credit sustained a high rate of growth of nominal aggregate demand and this was reflected in the balance-of-payments deficit of 1981 and the stabilization crisis of 1991.

In terms of infrastructural development and the provision of public goods, the record of the post-war governments is highly commendable. The economy's growth was enhanced by the provision of modern airport and harbour facilities and improved telecommunications in the market for tradables and tourism services. The post-independence demands of the electorate for social goods such as education, housing, health care and social security were met by increased levels of taxation and government borrowing. The post-independence governments were more committed to the idea of developing a modern welfare state than were the colonialists. Thus, education was made "free" up to tertiary level (see Howard 1992). The increased output of social goods led to an improvement in the income distribution.

In spite of the vast improvement in the output of public goods, the state's involvement in the economy was still restricted to a regulatory role. Some state ownership was achieved by the setting up of a marketing board, an agricultural corporation, two hotels, a national bank and the nationalizing of the bus transport system. The control of the key sectors of the economy such as agriculture, manufacturing and tourism was left to the private sector. Further, major public utilities such as electricity and telephone services remained in private sector hands. Successive governments paid lip service to local ownership and control, but localization and nationalization policies were never pursued as fundamental development strategies. We also showed the importance towards the end of the period of privatization and public sector reform in the process of structural adjustment.

Our analysis also demonstrates the important role played by the budget as an instrument of nominal income redistribution only toward the end of the review period. The colonial government was not concerned with direct income redistribution strategies through the use of the budget. The colonials pursued the goal of economic growth with the hope that some trickle down redistribution would be achieved. The redistribution strategy of the 1960s was concerned primarily with real income distribution by way of resource allocation policies to ensure an increased level of public goods. Direct nominal income redistribution through the budget was adopted in 1977 as a fundamental goal of policy. This was done primarily to reduce the welfare costs of the inflation tax. Budgetary redistribution was attempted by the modification of income tax brackets and rebates for lower income groups. It is true to say that during the 1960s and early 1970s, while budgetary policy tended to place particular emphasis on increased consumption taxes and other indirect taxes for financing purposes, budgetary policy between the late 1970s and 2000 was more concerned with nominal income redistribution.

ECONOMIC MANAGEMENT

Finally we need to comment briefly on the important role of management as a factor in the development of Barbados. The management of the Barbadian economy was reasonably efficient for most of the period before 2000, except for the highly aggressive fiscal policies of 1981 and 1991. The efficient management of Barbadian development was aided by certain "conditioning factors", a term borrowed from Musgrave (1969).

The first of these conditioning factors was the high level of political stability after World War II. A smooth transition from colonial rule to representative government and political independence was part of this process. Despite the consolidation of strong partisan loyalties after 1960, changes in government were not accompanied by civil strife. This political stability aided the implementation and operation of the foreign investment strategy and contributed to the transition to the tourism-based service economy of the 1980s.

Another important factor was the existence of a reasonably disciplined workforce and high levels of functional literacy among workers. This was aided by responsible trade union leadership. The manageability of the workforce contributed to increased productivity in various sectors of the economy. There was also some indication of improved human resource management to meet the demands of a computer-oriented information age after 1980.

Finally, a good internal and external communications network facilitated the functioning of the services economy, and enhanced the process of decision making. Improvements in airport and harbour facilities considerably accelerated the growth of offshore industry and tourism. These factors made it possible for the economy to cope with the demands of globalization.

The major policy implication of this study is that the future of the Barbadian economy lies in the development of services. Manufacturing must be geared to support the tourism sector, the most important of the internationally traded services. Further, data processing and other offshore financial business services offer some hope in the globalization era. The conditions that favoured raw material-based manufacturing in the 1960s, such as low wage costs, favourable external demand conditions and lower levels of international competition, were no longer present in 2000. The economy must therefore rely on the output of high quality services in a highly competitive world environment. Williams (2003) also discussed some of the financial challenges of globalization, including the need for financial service providers to absorb new technologies and compete internationally. The management of the service economy will require considerable collaboration between the public and private sectors.

Notes

CHAPTER 1

1. See Colonial Office 1945b, hereafter referred to as the Moyne Commission.
2. The summary discussion in the following two paragraphs is based on Starkey 1939:135–138; Colonial Office 1938, 1953b.
3. Our discussion of the tenantry system leans heavily on Marshall (with Marshall and Gibbs) 1977. See also "Analysis of the System of Plantation Tenantries", *Barbados Advocate*, 29 September 1980.
4. For instance, the Security of Tenure of Small Holdings Act 1955 and the Tenantries Control and Development Act 1965. These Acts gave greater security of tenure to tenants. The most significant piece of tenantries legislation was the Tenantries Freehold Purchase Act of 1980, which allowed tenants to purchase the house spots they were occupying.
5. For a discussion of the emergence of this elite see Karch 1979.

CHAPTER 2

1. For Lewis's theoretical model, see Lewis 1954; for the Puerto Rican model, see Lewis 1950.
2. The Best model referred to here is described in Best 1968. Our discussion of the size constraint draws on Demas 1965.
3. The Wicksell Lectures appeared in Lewis 1969 and the Janeway Lectures were reproduced in Lewis 1978.
4. For the ideas in this paragraph and the next, see Lewis 1955.

CHAPTER 3

1. See Jamaica Government 1945 as well as Colonial Office 1948.
2. See Colonial Office 1940.

CHAPTER 4

1. For a more detailed treatment of the growth problems of Barbados up to 1985, the reader is referred to Worrell 1987:52–78.
2. See *Barbados Advocate*, "1988 Statement of Financial and Budgetary Proposals", 29 April 1988.
3. Under this arrangement Barbados was granted the right to make purchases from the IMF in an amount equivalent to Special Drawing Rights (SDR) 31.875 million which was to be drawn in stages between 1 October 1982 and 31 May 1984.

CHAPTER 5

1. Our analysis in this section relies heavily on data from the Agricultural Censuses of 1946, 1961 and 1971. "Holdings without land" refers to farms kept by livestock farmers.
2. Farley (1964) reported that twelve estates out of a total of 240 were owned by non-Barbadians in 1962. McGregor et al. (1979) estimated that of the 132 estates in 1979 only four were foreign owned.
3. For this data see Department of Agriculture 1965.
4. For a detailed discussion of the historical background to the Commonwealth Sugar Agreement of 1951, see Mandeville 1961:1–4. Persaud (1973: 84–85) also analyses the quota agreements.
5. The details of the Lomé Convention of 1974 and its renewal in 1979 are set out in the *Courier*, no. 31 (March 1975) and no. 58 (November 1979).
6. The guaranteed price was negotiated annually within the range of prices in the European Community.
7. The 1942 Local Food Production and Defence Control Order made it necessary for inspectors to check that estates planted 12.5 percent of arable land in food crops.
8. This paragraph draws heavily from Barbados Sugar Producers' Association, *Barbados Sugar Industry Review,* no. 7 (March 1971).
9. The sources for the 1940 and 1948 data are *Barbados Blue Books* for 1940–46 and Colonial Office, *Colonial Reports* for 1947–51. The 1970s data were obtained from Barbados Ministry of Agriculture 1977c.
10. For example, the area under cotton declined from 1,096 acres in the period 1974–75 to 31 acres in the period 1975–76. One explanation is that private farmers reduced their acreage and switched back to sugar, hoping to benefit from higher prices. See Central Bank of Barbados (1976:13) for a discussion of the problems of the cotton industry. The reader is also referred to Barbados Ministry of Agriculture 1977a.
11. See Central Bank of Barbados, *Quarterly Report* 7, no. 2 (June 1980):15. One institutional reason advanced to explain this decline relates to the relaxation of the 1942 Local Food Production and Defence Control Order and the subsequent removal in 1970 of the food crop inspectors. The duty of the latter was to check whether plantations carried out the rule of 12.5 percent of arable land planted in food crops.
12. See Colonial Office, *Colonial Reports* for 1947–53. As early as 1947 schemes were considered to develop the fishing industry with CD and W grants. A loans scheme was inaugurated to enable fishers to build boats.
13. Shrimping was carried out under the aegis of the Barbados Sea Food Company, with 50 percent government participation. Most of the shrimp was shipped to markets in the United States.

CHAPTER 6

1. The problem of obtaining detailed analysis of value added in the manu-facturing sector in the 1960s stemmed from the fact that no output data on pioneer manufacturers for GDP purposes were readily available from the Department of Inland Revenue. These companies were non-taxable during the early years and the Department of Inland Revenue did not insist on their submitting their returns. See Barbados Statistical Service n.d.b.
2. These surveys covered 80 percent of the manufacturing sector. The surveys obtained employment data from enterprises that employed five or more people. See Barbados Statistical Service n.d.a.

CHAPTER 8

1. See *Official Gazette,* House of Assembly Debates (6 January 1947):23–28. Africa was being singled out as a possible area of settlement for coloured West Indians. See also *Report of the Joint Committee Appointed by the Two Houses of the Legislature to examine the Question of Over Population in Barbados and to make recommendations for dealing with the Problem* (Bridgetown, Barbados: Advocate Company, n.d.). This committee was set up in April 1952 to examine overpopulation.
2. See History Task Force 1979.
3. Contract emigration to the United States during the war was made possible through arrangements between the Anglo-American Caribbean Commis-sion and the American War Food Administration and War Manpower Commissions. For some details of actual numbers recruited during the war, see *Colonial Report* 1950:8.
4. Davison (1962:27) shows that about 40 percent of emigrants under the sponsored scheme between 1955 and 1960 worked with the London Trans-port Executive; 19 percent were hotel workers; 14 percent student nurses and 14 percent were employed at the British Transport Commission.
5. The data for this paragraph as well as the following were derived from *Barbados Economic Surveys* 1964–68.
6. For Jamaica, see Girling 1974. Girling analyses the extent to which migra-tion of human capital can reduce domestic economic growth. Migration cost analysis is also pursued by Palmer 1974.

References

Abdulah, N. 1977. *The Labour Force in the Commonwealth Caribbean: A Statistical Analysis*, St Augustine, Trinidad: University of the West Indies.

Adams, N. 1967. "Import Structure and Economic Growth: A Comparison of Cross Section and Time Series Data". *Economic Development and Cultural Change* 15, no. 2. part 1 (January).

———. 1968. "An Analysis of Food Consumption and Food Import Trends in Jamaica, 1950–1963". *Social and Economic Studies* 17, no. 1 (March).

———. 1971. "Import Structure and Economic Growth in Jamaica, 1954–64". *Social and Economic Studies* 20, no. 3.

Alleyne, P., and M. Howard. 2003. "An Assessment of the Operational Impact of the Barbados VAT between 1997 and 2001". *Journal of Eastern Caribbean Studies* 28, no. 1 (March).

Amin, S. 1974. *Accumulation on a World Scale: A Critique of the Theory of Underdevelopment*, vols. 1 and 2. New York: Monthly Review Press.

Aricanli, T., and D. Rodrik. 1990. "An Overview of Turkey's Experience with Economic Liberalization and Structural Adjustment". *World Development* 18, no. 10.

Armstrong, W., E. Daniel and A.A. Francis. 1974. "Structural Analysis of the Barbados Economy 1968 with an Application to the Tourist Industry". *Social and Economic Studies* 23, no. 4.

Baer, W., and M.E. Herve. 1966. "Employment and Industrialization in Developing Countries". *Quarterly Journal of Economics* 80.

Barbados Development Bank. Various years (1957–58, 1969–80). *Annual Reports*.

Barbados Government. 1945. *A Ten-Year Plan for Barbados: Sketch Plan of Development 1946–1956*. Bridgetown, Barbados: Advocate Co.

———. 1953. *Five-Year Plan of Development and Taxation*. Bridgetown, Barbados: Advocate Co.

———. 1955–60. *Barbados Development Plan*. Bridgetown, Barbados: Government Printing Office.

———. 1960–65. *Barbados Development Plan*. Bridgetown, Barbados: Government Printing Office.

———. 1965–68. *Barbados Development Plan*. Bridgetown, Barbados: Government Printing Office.

———. 1969–72. *Barbados Development Plan*. Bridgetown, Barbados: Government Printing Office.

———. 1973–77. *Barbados Development Plan*. Bridgetown, Barbados: Government Printing Office.

———. 1979–83. *Barbados Development Plan*. Bridgetown, Barbados: Government Printing Office.

———. Various years (1964–85). *Economic Surveys*. Bridgetown, Barbados: Government Printing Office.

———. Department of Labour. Various years (1946–75). *Annual Reports.*

———. House of Assembly. 1947. *Official Gazette.* Bridgetown, Barbados: Government Printing Office.

———. House of Assembly. 1950. *Official Gazette.* Bridgetown, Barbados: Government Printing Office.

———. Inland Revenue. 1955–60. *Annual Reports.* Bridgetown, Barbados: Commissioner of Inland Revenue.

Barbados Industrial Development Corporation. Various years (1969–80 and 1996–2001). *Annual Reports.* Bridgetown, Barbados.

Barbados Ministry of Agriculture. 1946. *Census of Agriculture.* Bridgetown, Barbados: Ministry of Agriculture.

———. 1961. *Census of Agriculture.* Bridgetown, Barbados: Ministry of Agriculture.

———. 1971. *Census of Agriculture.* Bridgetown, Barbados: Ministry of Agriculture.

———. 1977a. *Profiles of Agricultural Development in Barbados, Report no. 3: Opportunities for Production and Farming.* Bridgetown, Barbados: United Nations Development Programme/Food and Agricultural Organization.

———. 1977b. *Profiles of Agricultural Development in Barbados, Report no. 4: Opportunities for Livestock and Animal Feed Production.* Bridgetown, Barbados: United Nations Development Programme/Food and Agricultural Organization.

———. 1977c. *Profiles of Agricultural Development in Barbados, Report no. 5: Food Supply and Nutrition.* Bridgetown, Barbados: United Nations Development Programme/Food and Agricultural Organization.

———. 1978. *Barbados Agricultural Statistics,* vol. 2, October. Bridgetown, Barbados: Ministry of Agriculture.

———. 2002a. *Regional Special Programme for Food Security,* Project TCP/RLA/0174, written by G.C.E. Rawlins. Bridgetown, Barbados: Food and Agriculture Organization.

———. 2002b. *Small Island Developing States and Multilateral Agricultural Liberalization,* written by G.C.E. Rawlins. Bridgetown, Barbados: United Nations Conference on Trade and Development.

———. 2002c. *Strategic Plan for the Agricultural Sector in Barbados 2002–2012.* Bridgetown, Barbados: Ministry of Agriculture.

Barbados Ministry of Finance. Various years (1967–85). *Financial Statement and Budgetary Proposal.* Bridgetown, Barbados: Ministry of Finance.

———. 1987. *Barbados Economic Report.* Bridgetown, Barbados: Ministry of Finance.

Barbados Statistical Service. 1960. *A Study of the National Income of Barbados 1956–1959.* Bridgetown, Barbados: Barbados Statistical Service.

———. 1963. *National Income and Product 1960–62.* Bridgetown, Barbados: Barbados Statistical Service.

———. 1965. *Abstract of Statistics,* no. 5. Bridgetown, Barbados: Barbados Statistical Service.

———. Various years (1971–85). *Survey of Industrial Establishments.* Bridgetown, Barbados: Barbados Statistical Service.

———. Various years (1974–77). *Annual Overseas Trade Report.* Bridgetown, Barbados: Barbados Statistical Service.

———. 1977. *Financial Statistics*, no. 5, 1966–76. Bridgetown, Barbados: Barbados Statistical Service.

———. 1994. *Industrial Census*. Bridgetown, Barbados: Barbados Statistical Service.

———. 2001. *Digest of Tourism Statistics*. Bridgetown, Barbados: Barbados Statistical Service.

———. n.d.a. *Survey of Secondary Manufacturing Establishments, 1957–1958*. Bridgetown, Barbados: Government Printing Office.

———. n.d.b. "National Income and Product 1960–1962 with Provisional Estimates for 1963 and 1964". Mimeo.

———. n.d.c. "Report on a Survey of Secondary Establishments, 1975–1985". Mimeo.

Barbados Sugar Producers' Association. Various years (1969–80). *Barbados Sugar Industry Review*. Bridgetown, Barbados: Barbados Sugar Producers' Association.

Barrow, C., and E. Greene. 1979. *Small Business in Barbados: A Case of Survival*. Cave Hill, Barbados: Institute of Social and Economic Research, University of the West Indies.

Bauer, P.T., and B.S. Yamey. 1965. "Economic Progress and Occupational Distribution". In *Studies in Economic Development*, edited by B. Okun and R.W. Richards. New York: Holt, Rinehart and Winston.

Beasley, C.G. 1952. *A Fiscal Survey of Barbados*. Bridgetown, Barbados: Cole's Printery.

Beckford, G.L. 1968. "Towards an Appropriate Theoretical Framework for Agricultural Development Planning and Policy". *Social and Economic Studies* 17, no. 3 (September).

———. 1969. "The Economics of Agricultural Resource Use and Development in Plantation Economies". *Social and Economic Studies* 18, no. 4 (December).

———. 1972. *Persistent Poverty*. New York: Oxford University Press.

Beckles, H. 1989. *Corporate Power in Barbados: The Mutual Affair; Economic Injustice in a Political Democracy*. Bridgetown, Barbados: Lighthouse Communications.

———. 2004. *Chattel House Blues: The Making of a Democratic Society in Barbados from Clement Payne to Owen Arthur*. Kingston: Ian Randle.

Belgrave, A., and K. Greenidge. 2003. "Financial Liberalization and the Challenges for Policy-Makers in Developing Countries". In *Facing Globalisation, Impact and Challenges for Barbados and the Caribbean*, edited by H. Codrington, R. Craigwell and D. Downes. Bridgetown, Barbados: Central Bank of Barbados.

Belgrave, A., and W. Ward. 1997. *Foreign Direct Investment and the Barbadian Economy*. Working Papers, no. 2. Bridgetown, Barbados: Central Bank of Barbados.

Belle, G.A. 1974. "The Political Economy of Barbados 1937–1946: 1966–1972". MSc thesis, Department of Government, University of the West Indies, Mona.

Benn, D. 1974. "The Theory of Plantation Economy and Society: A Methodological Critique". *Journal of Commonwealth and Comparative Politics* 12 (November).

Bernal, R. 2000. "Globalization and Small Developing Countries: The Imperative for Repositioning". In *Globalization a Calculus of Inequality: Perspectives from the South*, edited by D. Benn and K. Hall. Kingston: Ian Randle.

Bernal, R., M. Figuero and M. Witter. 1984. "Caribbean Economic Thought: The Critical Tradition". *Social and Economic Studies* 33, no. 2.

Best, L. 1968. "A Model of Pure Plantation Economy". *Social and Economic Studies* 17, no. 3 (September).

―――. 1971. "Size and Survival". In *Readings in the Political Economy of the Caribbean*, edited by N. Girvan and O. Jefferson. Kingston: New World Group.

―――. 1980. "International Cooperation in the Industrialization Process: The Case of Trinidad and Tobago". In *Industry 2000*. New York: United Nations.

Bethel, J. 1960. "A National Accounts Study of the Economy of Barbados". *Social and Economic Studies* 9, no. 2 (June).

Bhagwati, A.W., and P. Desai. 1970. *India, Planning for Industrialization: Industrialization and Trade Policies since 1951*. London: Oxford University Press.

Bhalla, A.S. 1985. *Technology and Employment in Industry*. Geneva: International Labour Organization.

Bishop, M., R. Corbin and N. Duncan. 1998. "Barbados: Social Development in a Small Island State". In *Development with a Human Face*, edited by S. Mehrotra and R. Jolly. Oxford: Clarendon Press.

Blackman, C.N. 1979. "The Economic Development of Small Countries". In *Contemporary International Relations of the Caribbean*, edited by B. Ince. St Augustine, Trinidad: University of the West Indies.

―――. 1987. "Speech to the Rotary Club on Barbadian Economy". *Nation* (2 December).

―――. 2001. "Towards a Barbados National Strategic Plan, 2001–2010". Paper Commissioned by the Rt. Honourable Owen S. Arthur, Prime Minister of Barbados, February.

Boamah, D. 1985. "Wage Formation, Employment and Output in Barbados". *Social and Economic Studies* 34, no. 4.

―――. 1996. "Savings and Investment in the Barbados Economy (1965–1990)". *Central Bank of Barbados Economic Review* 23, no. 1 (June).

Boamah, D., S. Byron and C Maxwell. 2003. "Examining the Impact of Taxation on Income Distribution in Barbados". Mimeo, Central Bank of Barbados.

Bonnett, R.L. 1956. "The National Income and National Accounts of Barbados". *Social and Economic Studies* 5, no. 3 (September).

―――. 1975. "Built-in Flexibility of Individual Income Taxation in an Underdeveloped Country: A Case Study of Barbados". *C.S.O. Research Papers*, no. 8.

Bourne, C. 1974. "The Political Economy of Indigenous Commercial Banking in Guyana". *Social and Economic Studies* 23, no. 1 (March).

Brett, E.A. 1973. *Colonialism and Underdevelopment in East Africa: The Politics of Economic Change, 1919–1939*. New York: Nok Publishers.

Brewster, H., and Thomas, C.Y. 1967. *The Dynamics of West Indian Economic Integration*. Kingston: Institute of Social and Economic Research, University of the West Indies.

British Development in the Caribbean. 1968. *West Indian Census of Agriculture 1961*. Bridgetown, Barbados: Government Printing Office.

Brookfield, H. 1979. "Planning for Island Development". Paper presented at Conference on Inter-Island Shipping, Singapore, 10–16 June.

Bryden, J.M. 1975. *Tourism and Development: A Case Study of the Commonwealth Caribbean*. Cambridge: Cambridge University Press.

Bryden, J.M., and M. Faber. 1971. "Multiplying the Tourist Multiplier". *Social and Economic Studies* 20, no. 1 (March).

Caribbean Commission. 1949. *The Development of Primary and Secondary Industries in the Caribbean Area: Development and Welfare in the West Indies*, Bulletin no. 27.

Caribbean Development Bank (CDB). 1972. "Statement by the President, Sir Arthur Lewis". Second Annual Meeting of the Board of Governors, St Lucia, 21 April.

CARICOM Secretariat. 2000. *Caribbean Trade and Investment Report 2000*. Kingston: Ian Randle.

Carter, A. 1997. "Economic Size, Openness and Export Diversification: A Statistical Analysis". *Central Bank of Barbados Economic Review* 24, no. 3 (December).

Central Bank of Barbados. Various years (1974–2002). *Economic and Financial Statistics*. Bridgetown, Barbados: Central Bank of Barbados.

———. Various years (1974–2001). *Quarterly Reports and Economic Review*. Bridgetown, Barbados: Central Bank of Barbados.

———. Various years (1976–2002). *Annual Statistical Digests*. Bridgetown, Barbados: Central Bank of Barbados.

———. Various years (1976–2002). *Balance of Payments of Barbados*. Bridgetown, Barbados: Central Bank of Barbados.

Chandarvarkar, A.G. 1971. "Some Aspects of Interest Rate Policies in Less Developed Countries". *IMF Staff Papers* 28, no. 1 (March).

Charles, S. 1994. *The Services Sector in the Caribbean Economies: Some Development and Management Issues*. Cave Hill, Barbados: Institute for Social and Economic Research.

Chelliah, R.J. 1971. "Trends in Taxation in Developing Countries". *IMF Staff Papers* 18 (July).

Chenery, H.B. 1960. "Patterns of Industrial Development". *American Economic Review* (September).

Chenery, H.B., and M. Syrquin. 1975. *Patterns of Development*. Oxford: Oxford University Press.

Clarke, C. 1957. *The Conditions of Economic Progress*. London: Macmillan.

Clarke, C., C. Wood and D. Worrell. 1986. "Prices, Incomes and the Growth of Tourism in Barbados, 1956–83". *Central Bank of Barbados Economic Review* 13, no. 1 (June).

Clarkson, B., and R. Craigwell. 1997. *An Analysis of the Service Sector in Barbados*. Working Papers, no. 2. Bridgetown, Barbados: Central Bank of Barbados.

Codrington, H. 1987. "Foreign Investment in the Private Sector of Barbados, 1956–1985". *Central Bank of Barbados Economic Review* 14, no. 1 (14–29 June).

Codrington, H., R. Craigwell and C. Haynes, eds. 1997. *Central Banking in Barbados: Reflections and Challenges*. Bridgetown, Barbados: Central Bank of Barbados.

Codrington, H., and C. Holder. 1984. "The Terms of Trade Experience of Barbados and Trinidad and Tobago 1955-1980". *Central Bank of Barbados Economic Review* 11, no. 1 (June).

Codrington, V.B. 1978. "Land Utilization and Economic Development: A Case Study of Barbados 1900–1976". Mimeo, Institute of Social and Economic Research, University of the West Indies, Cave Hill, Barbados.

Colonial Office. Great Britain. 1938. *Colonial Report of Barbados 1936–1937*. London: HMSO.

———. 1940. *Statement of Policy on Colonial Development and Welfare*, Cmd. 6175. London: HMSO.

————. 1945a. *Development and Welfare in the West Indies, 1943–1944*, no. 189. London: HMSO.

————. 1945b. *Report of the West India Royal Commission*. London: HMSO.

————. 1947a. *The Colonial Empire 1939–1947*, Cmd. 7167. London: HMSO.

————. 1947b. *Development and Welfare in the West Indies 1945–1946*, no. 212. London: HMSO.

————. 1948. *Report by British Member of the Industrial Survey Panel appointed by the Caribbean Commission. Industrial Development in the British Territories of the Caribbean* (Galloti Report, June). London: HMSO.

————. 1952. *Colonial Report of Barbados 1950–1951*. London: HMSO.

————. 1953a. *An Economic Survey of the Colonial Empire 1937*. London: HMSO.

————. 1953b. *An Economic Survey of the Colonial Territories*. London: HMSO.

————. 1953c. *Industrial Development in Jamaica, Trinidad, Barbados and British Guyana. Report of Mission of United Kingdom Industrialists*, October–November 1952, no. 294. London: HMSO.

Coppin, A. 1995. "Female Participation in Barbados' Labour Market: A Post-Independence Perspective". *Central Bank of Barbados Economic Review* 22, no. 1.

Cox, M. 1978. "The Distribution of Income in Barbados". Mimeo, Institute of Social and Economic Research, University of the West Indies, Cave Hill, Barbados.

Cox, W. 1987. "The Manufacturing Sector in the Economy of Barbados, 1946–1980". In *The Economy of Barbados, 1946–1980*, edited by D. Worrell. Bridgetown, Barbados: Central Bank of Barbados.

Cox, W., and D. Worrell. 1978. "Import Structure and Economic Growth in Barbados 1957–1977". Mimeo, Central Bank of Barbados.

Craigwell, R., D. Downes and M. Howard. 2001. "The Finance-Growth Nexus: A Multivariate VAR Analysis of Small Open Economy". *Savings and Development*, no. 2.

Craigwell, R.C., and C. Grandbois. 1999. "The Performance of the Securities Exchange of Barbados". *Savings and Development*, no. 4.

Craigwell, R.C., and D. Lewis. 1998. "The Determinants of Growth in Small Open Economy: Barbados". *Journal of Eastern Caribbean Studies* 23, no. 2 (June).

Craigwell, R., and A. Warner. 2003. "Labour Market Dynamics in Barbados: Policies and Implications of Globalization". In *Facing Globalization: Impact and Challenges for Barbados and the Caribbean*, edited by A. Codrington et al. Bridgetown, Barbados: Central Bank of Barbados.

Cumberbatch, C. 1997. "A Model of Inflation in Barbados". In *Macroeconomics and Finance in the Caribbean: Quantitative Analyses*, edited by D. Worrell and R. Craigwell. Port of Spain, Trinidad: Caribbean Centre for Monetary Studies.

Cumper, G.E. 1957. "Working Class Emigration from Barbados to U.K. October 1955". *Social and Economic Studies* 6, no. 1 (March).

————. 1959. "Employment in Barbados". *Social and Economic Studies* 8, no. 2 (June).

————. 1960. "Personal Consumption in the West Indies". In *The Economy of the West Indies*, edited by G. E. Cumper. Kingston: Institute of Social and Economic Studies, University of the West Indies.

David, W.L. 1970. "Public Savings and Investment in the Caribbean: A Study of Selected Caribbean Countries". *Caribbean Studies* 10, no. 1 (April).

Davison, R.B. 1962. *West Indian Migrants*. London: Oxford University Press.

DeCaires, C. 1999. "Foreign Sales Corporations". In *Business Barbados*. St James, Barbados: Miller Publishing.

Demas, W. 1965. *The Economics of Development in Small Countries with Special Reference to the Caribbean*. Montreal: McGill University Press.

Department of Agriculture. 1965. *A Digest of West Indian Agricultural Statistics*. St Augustine, Trinidad: (Department of Agriculture, University of the West Indies.

Desai, P. 1969. "Alternative Measures of Import Substitution". *Oxford Economic Papers* 21, no. 3 (November).

Diaz-Alejandro, C.F. 1965. "Industrialization and Labour Productivity Differentials". *Review of Economics and Statistics* 47, no. 2 (May).

Diez de Medina, R. 1997. "Poverty and Income Distribution in Barbados 1996". Mimeo, Inter-American Development Bank, Washington, DC.

Downes, A. 1985. "Industrial Growth and Employment in a Small Developing Country: The Case of Barbados, 1955–1980". PhD thesis, University of Manchester.

———. 1987. "The Distribution of Household Income in Barbados". *Social and Economic Studies* 36, no. 4 (December).

———. 1994. "The Impact of the Prices and Incomes Policy on the Economic Climate of Barbados". *Social and Economic Studies* 43, no. 4 (December).

Downes, A., C. Holder and H. Leon. 1990. "The Wage-Price-Productivity Relationship in a Small Developing Country: The Case of Barbados". *Social and Economic Studies* 39, no. 2 (June).

———. 1991. "A Cointegration Approach to Modelling Inflation in a Small Open Economy". *Journal of Economic Development* 16, no. 1 (June).

Downes, A.S., and A.W.A. McClean. 1982. "Wage Determination in a Small Open Unionized Economy: The Case of Barbados". Mimeo, University of the West Indies, Cave Hill, Barbados.

Doxey, G. and Associates. 1971. *The Tourist Industry in Barbados*. Kitchener: Dusco Graphics.

Doyle, M., and A. Johnson. 1999. "Does Offshore Business Mean Onshore Economic Gains". Paper presented at Annual Review Seminar, Central Bank of Barbados, Bridgetown, Barbados, July.

Dunning, J.H. 1997. *Alliance Capitalism and Global Business*. London: Routledge.

Ecevit, Z., and K. Zachariah. 1978. "International Labour Migration". *Finance and Development* 15, no. 4 (December).

Emtage, S.E. 1969. "Growth Development and Planning in a Small Economy: The Case of Barbados". MPhil thesis, Sussex University.

Evans, C. 1999. "Captive Insurance in Barbados". In *Business Barbados*. St James, Barbados: Miller Publishing.

Evans, P. 1979. *Dependent Development: The Alliance of Multinational, State and Local Capital in Brazil*. Princeton, NJ: Princeton University Press.

Fabozzi, F.J., et al. 1994. *Foundations of Financial Markets and Institutions*. Upper Saddle River, NJ: Prentice Hall.

Fama, E. 1970. "Efficient Capital Markets: A Review of Theory and Empirical Work". *Journal of Finance* 25, no. 2.

Farley, R. 1964. *Report of the Commission of Enquiry into the Barbados Sugar Industry 1962–1963*. Bridgetown, Barbados: Government Printing Office.

Fisher, A.G.B. 1939. "Production, Primary, Secondary and Tertiary". *Economic Record* (June).

Food and Agricultural Organization (FAO). 1978. "Profiles of Agricultural Development: Food Supply and Nutrition". Mimeo, Project Bar 73/005, Ministry of Agriculture, Bridgetown, Barbados.

Frank, A.G. 1972. "Sociology of Development and Underdevelopment of Sociology". In *Dependence and Underdevelopment. Latin America's Political Economy*, edited by J.D. Crokroft, A.G. Frank and D. Johnson. New York: Doubleday.

Gafar, J. 1974. "The Terms of Trade Experience of the Caribbean Common Market Countries". *C.S.O. Research Papers*, no. 7.

Gafar, J., and W. Joefield-Napier. 1978. *Trends and Patterns of Caribbean Trade 1954–1970*. Kingston: Institute of Social and Economic Research, University of the West Indies.

Galbis, V. 1979. "Inflation and Interest Rate Policies in Latin America 1967–1976". *IMF Staff Papers* 26, no. 2 (June).

Galtung, J. 1976. "The Lomé Convention and Neo-Capitalism". *African Review* 6, no. 1.

Girling, R.K. 1974. "The Migration of Human Capital from the Third World: The Implications and Some Data on the Jamaican Case". *Social and Economic Studies* 23, no. 1 (March).

Girvan, N. 1971a. "Making the Rules of the Game: Country–Company Agreements in the Bauxite Industry". *Social and Economic Studies* 20, no. 4 (December).

———. 1971b. "Why We Need to Nationalize Bauxite and How". In *Readings in the Political Economy of the Caribbean*, edited by N. Girvan and O. Jefferson. Kingston: New World Group.

———. 1973. "The Development of Dependency Economics in the Caribbean and Latin America". *Social and Economic Studies* 22, no. 1 (March).

———. 2000. "Globalization and Counter-Globalization: The Caribbean in the Context of the South". In *Globalization: A Calculus of Inequality*, edited by D. Benn and K. Hall. Kingston: Ian Randle.

———. 2002. "Notes for a Retrospective on the Theory of Plantation Economy of Lloyd Best and Kari Polanyi Levitt". In *Caribbean Economics and Global Restructuring*, edited by M. Derné and K. Nurse. Kingston: Ian Randle.

Goldsmith, R. 1969. *Financial Structure and Development*. New Haven, CT: Yale University Press.

Gonzales, A. 1976. "Trade Strategies of the Commonwealth Caribbean in a Changing World Economic Order: Special Reference to the Lomé Convention and Caribbean Economic Integration". In *Caribbean Year Book of International Relations*, edited by L. Manigat. Port of Spain, Trinidad: Institute of International Relations, University of the West Indies.

Grassman, S. 1980. "Long Term Trends in Openness of National Economies". *Oxford Economic Papers* 32, no. 1 (March).

Griffith, J. 2000. *The Impact of VAT on Tourism in Barbados*. Working Papers. Bridgetown, Barbados: Central Bank of Barbados.

Harewood, J. 1972. "Changes in the Demand for and Supply of Labour in the Caribbean 1946–1960". *Social and Economic Studies* 21, no. 1 (March).

Haynes, C. 1997. "Lessons from Barbados' Experiment with the International Monetary Fund". In *Central Banking in Barbados: Reflections and Challenges*, edited by H. Codrington, R. Craigwell and C. Haynes. Bridgetown, Barbados: Central Bank of Barbados.

History Task Force, Centro de Estudios Puertorriqueños, City University of New York. 1979. *Labour Migration under Capitalism*. New York: Monthly Review Press.

Holder, C., and R. Prescod. 1984. "Income Distribution in Barbados", Mimeo, Central Bank of Barbados.

Holder, J. 1978. "The Impact of the Energy Crisis 1973/74 on Tourism and Some Consequences for Caribbean Development". Paper presented at the Caribbean Conference on Energy for Development, Puerto Rico, April.

Holder, L. 1982. "Tax Revenue Performance in Barbados". Mimeo, Central Bank of Barbados.

Howard, M. 1976. "Interest Rate Behaviour in an Open Developing Economy: The Case of Barbados 1960–1976". *Quarterly Report* [Central Bank of Barbados] 3, no. 4 (December).

———. 1979a. *The Fiscal System of Barbados 1946–1965*, Occasional Papers Series, no. 12, Cave Hill, Barbados: Institute of Social and Economic Research, University of the West Indies.

———. 1979b. "A Preliminary Investigation into the Demand for Money in Barbados 1960–1976". *Social and Economic Studies* 28, no. 4 (December).

———. 1980. "A Note on the Cost and Revenue Structure of Commercial Banks in Barbados". *Social and Economic Studies* 29, no. 2 (June).

———. 1987. "Barbados: Income Tax Reform: An Analysis of Two Budgets in 1986". *Bulletin for International Fiscal Documentation* (April).

———. 1989. *Dependence and Development in Barbados, 1945–1985*, Bridgetown, Barbados: Carib Research and Publications.

———. 1992. *Public Finance in Small Open Economies: The Caribbean Experience*. Westport, CT: Praeger.

———. 2001a. "Financial Liberalization in Jamaica". *Savings and Development*, no. 4.

———. 2001b. *Public Sector Economics for Developing Countries*. Kingston: University of the West Indies Press.

———. 2002. "Another Look at Wagner's Law in Small Economies". *Journal of Eastern Caribbean Studies* 27, no. 1 (March).

Howard, M., and B. Wapensky. 1974. "Commercial Bank Liquidity and Central Bank Operations in Barbados". *Quarterly Report* [Central Bank of Barbados] 1, no 3 (December).

Ingham, B. 1993. "The Meaning of Development: Interactions between "New" and "Old" Ideas. *World Development* 21, no. 11 (November).

Inter-American Development Bank (IADB). 1978. *Economic and Social Progress in Latin America*. Washington, DC: IADB.

International Monetary Fund (IMF). 1950. *Annual Report*. Washington, DC: IMF.

Jamaica Government. 1945. *Report of the Economic Policy Committee* (Benham Report). Kingston: Government Printer.

———. 1946. *West Indian Census 1946*, vol. 1, Parts A and B. Kingston: Central Bureau of Statistics.

Jefferson, O. 1971. *The Post-War Economic Development of Jamaica*. Kingston: Institute of Social and Economic Research, University of the West Indies.

Johnson, H. 1977. "The West Indies and the Conversion of the British Official Classes to the Development Idea". *Journal of Commonwealth and Comparative Politics* 15, no. 1.

Karch, C. 1979. "The Transformation and Consolidation of the Corporate Plantation Economy in Barbados: 1960–1977". PhD thesis, Rutgers University.

Karch, C. (with H. Carter). 1997. *The Rise of the Phoenix: The Barbados Mutual Life Assurance Society in Caribbean Economy and Society, 1840–1890*. Kingston: Ian Randle.

Khalaf, N. 1976. "Country Size and Economic Instability". *Journal of Development Studies* 12, no. 4 (July).

Khatkate, D., and K. Riechel. 1980. "Multipurpose Banking: Its Nature, Scope and Relevance for Less Developed Countries". *IMF Staff Papers* 27, no. 3 (September).

Klak, T. 1998. "Thirteen Theses on Globalisation and Neoliberalism". In *Globalisation and Neoliberalism: The Caribbean Context*, edited by T. Klak. Lanham, MD: Rowman and Littlefield.

Kuznets, S. 1963. "Economic Growth of Small Nations". In *Economic Consequences of the Size of Nations*, edited by E.A.G. Robinson. London: Macmillan.

Lary, H.B. 1968. *Imports of Manufactures from Less Developed Countries*. New York: National Bureau of Economic Research.

Lashley, J. 2002. "Survey of Barbadian Business: Main Findings and Issues". Mimeo. Sir Arthur Lewis Institute of Social and Economic Studies, Cave Hill, Barbados.

Lee, J.M. 1967. *Colonial Development and Good Government*. Oxford: Clarendon Press.

Levitt, E., and I. Gulati. 1970. "Income Effect of Tourist Spending: Mystification Multiplied: A Critical Comment on the Zinder Report". *Social and Economic Studies* 9, no. 3 (September).

Levitt, K., and M. Witter, eds. 1996. *The Critical Tradition of Caribbean Political Economy: The Legacy of George Beckford*. Kingston: Ian Randle.

Lewis, G.K. 1968. *The Growth of the Modern British West Indies*. New York: Monthly Review Press.

Lewis, W.A. 1936. "The Evolution of the Peasantry in the British West Indies". Mimeo, University of the West Indies Library.

———. 1937. *Labour in the West Indies: The Birth of a Workers' Movement*. London: New Beacon Books.

———. 1950. "Industrialization of the British West Indies". *Caribbean Economic Review* 2, no. 1.

———. 1954. "Economic Development with Unlimited Supplies of Labour". *Manchester School* 22.

———. 1955. *The Theory of Economic Growth*. London: Allen and Unwin.

———. 1969. *Aspects of Tropical Trade*. Stockholm: Amquist and Wicksell.

———. 1972. "Reflections on Unlimited Labour". In *International Economics and Development*, edited by L. Dimarco. London: Academic Press.

———. 1976. "Development and Distribution". In *Employment, Income Distribution and Development Strategy,* edited by A. Cairncross and M. Puri. London: Macmillan.

———. 1978. *The Evolution of the International Economic Order.* Princeton, NJ: Princeton University Press.

Lewis-Bynoe, D.A., J. Griffith, W. Moore and G. Rawlins. 2000. "The Impact of Trade Liberalisation on Specific Sectors of the Barbados Economy and Consumers". *Central Bank of Barbados Economic Review* 27 (June).

Little, I., T. Scitovsky and M. Scott. 1970. *Industry and Trade in Some Developing Countries.* London: Oxford University Press.

Lynch, R. 1995. *Gender Segregation in the Barbadian Labour Market, 1946 and 1980.* Kingston: Consortium Graduate School of Social Sciences.

Maizels, A. 1968. *Exports and Economic Growth of Developing Countries.* Cambridge: Cambridge University Press.

Mandeville, R.G.F. 1961. "The Commonwealth Sugar Agreement (A Brief Explanations of Its Provisions". *Barbados Sugar Industry Review,* no. 1. Bridgetown, Barbados: Barbados Sugar Producers' Association.

Marshall, D.I. 1977. *Tourism and Employment in Barbados.* Occasional Papers Series, 6. Cave Hill, Barbados: Institute of Social and Economic Research, University of the West Indies.

Marshall, W.K. (with T. Marshall and B. Gibbs). 1977. "The Establishment of a Peasantry in Barbados 1840–1920". Mimeo, Department of History, University of the West Indies, Cave Hill, Barbados.

Mascoll, C. 1985. "Wages, Productivity and Employment in Barbados 1949–1982". *Economic Review* 12, no. 3 (December).

———. 1991. "Trends in Representative Tax Rates of Representative Individuals in Barbados during the 1980s". *Central Bank of Barbados Economic Review* 18, no. 3.

Maude, J. 1949. *Report of Local Government in Barbados.* Bridgetown, Barbados: Advocate Co.

McClean, A.W.A. 1975. *Money and Banking in the East Caribbean Currency Area.* Kingston: Institute of Social and Economic Research, University of the West Indies.

McGregor, A., et al. 1979. *The Barbados Sugar Industry.* Bridgetown, Barbados: Government Printing Office.

McIntyre, A. 1971. "Some Issues in Trade Policy in the West Indies". In *Readings in Political Economy of the Caribbean,* edited by N. Girvan and O. Jefferson. Kingston: New World Group.

McIntyre, A., and B. Watson. 1970. *Studies in Foreign Investment in the Commonwealth Caribbean, no. 1, Trinidad and Tobago.* Kingston: Institute of Social and Economic Research, University of the West Indies.

McKenzie, A.F. 1958. *Report of an Inquiry into the Sugar Industry of Barbados.* Bridgetown, Barbados: Government Printing Office.

Musgrave, R. 1969. *Fiscal Systems.* New Haven, Connecticut: Yale University Press.

Nabudere, D. 1976. "The Lomé Convention and the Consolidation of Neo-Colonialism". *African Review* 6, no. 3.

Nicholls, C. 1999. "International Business Companies (IBCs)". In *Business Barbados.* St James, Barbados: Miller Publishing.

North, D. 1989. "Institutions and Economic Growth". *World Development* 17, no. 9.

Nurse, L.L. 1979. "Residential Subdivision of Barbados 1965–1977". MPhil thesis, University of Edinburgh.

Palmer, R. 1979. *Caribbean Dependence on the United States Economy.* New York: Praeger.

Palmer, R.W. 1974. "A Decade of West Indian Migration in the USA, 1962–1972: An Economic Analysis". *Social and Economic Studies* 23, no. 4 (December).

Passaris, C.E. 1979. "Absorptive Capacity and Canada's Post-War Immigration Policy". *International Integration* 17, no. 3.

Patrick, H.T. 1966. "Financial Development and Economic Growth in Underdeveloped Countries". *Economic Development and Cultural Change* 14.

Pearce, D., and J. Warford. 1993. *World without End: Economics, Environment and Sustainable Development: A Summary.* Washington, DC: World Bank.

Pechman, J.A. 1956. "Yield of the Individual Income Tax during a Recession". In *Policies to Combat Depression.* Princeton, NJ: National Bureau for Economic Research.

Persaud, B. 1973. "An Economic Study of the Barbados Sugar Industry". PhD thesis, Reading University.

Persaud, B., and L. Persaud. 1968. "The Impact of Agricultural Diversification Policies in Barbados in the Post-War Period". *Social and Economic Studies* 17, no. 3 (September).

Phillips, E. 1977. "Financial Aspects of the Barbados Sugar Industry". In *Quarterly Report* [Central Bank of Barbados] 4, no. 4 (December).

———. 1982. "The Development of the Tourist Industry in Barbados 1956–1980". In *The Economy of Barbados 1946–1980*, edited by D. Worrell. Bridgetown, Barbados: Central Bank of Barbados.

Prachouny, M. 1975. *Small Open Economies.* London: D.C. Heath.

Rodrik, D. 1990. "How Should Structural Adjustment Programmes Be Designed?" *World Development* 18, no. 7.

———. 2000. *Institutions for High Quality Growth. What they Are and How to Acquire Them.* National Bureau of Economic Research, Working Paper no. W 1540. Cambridge: John F. Kennedy School of Government, Harvard University.

———. 2002. *Feasible Globalizations.* Harvard University Working Paper. May. Cambridge: Harvard University.

Schoen, C. 1996. "Barbados FSC's Increase in Popularity". *Barbados International Business Report*, no. 9 (Summer).

Seers, D. 1979. "The Meaning of Development" and "Postscript: The New Meaning of Development". In *Development Theory*, edited by D. Lehmann. London: Frank Cass.

Sen, A. 1988. "The Concept of Development". In *Handbook of Development Economics*, edited by H. Chenery and T.N. Srinivasan. Amsterdam: Elsevier.

Shankland Cox Partnership. 1974. *Tourism Supply in the Caribbean Region.* Washington, DC: World Bank.

Skeete, R., K. Coppin and D. Boamah. 2003. "Elasticities and Buoyancies of the Barbados Tax System, 1977–1999". Mimeo, Central Bank of Barbados.

Smith, I. 1976. "Can the West Indies Sugar Industry Survive?" *Oxford Bulletin of Economics and Statistics* 38 (May).

Starkey, O.P. 1939. *The Economic Geography of Barbados*. New York, Columbia University Press.

Straughn, R. 2000. *Constructing and Using International Trade Prices Indices in Barbados*. Working Papers. Bridgetown, Barbados: Central Bank of Barbados.

Straw, K.H. 1954. "Budgets and Nutrition in Barbados". *Social and Economic Studies* 3, no. 1 (June).

———. 1954. "A Survey of Income and Consumption Patterns in Barbados". *Social and Economic Studies* 1, no. 4.

Sudama, T. 1979. "The Model of Plantation Economy: The Case of Trinidad and Tobago". *Latin American Perspectives* 5, no. 1 (Winter).

Tanzi, V., and H. Zee. 1997. "Fiscal Policy and Long-Run Growth". *International Monetary Fund Staff Papers* 44, no. 2 (June).

Thomas, C.Y. 1965. *Monetary and Financial Arrangements in a Dependent Monetary Economy*. Kingston: Institute of Social and Economic Research, University of the West Indies.

———. 1974. *Dependence and Transformation*. New York: Monthly Review Press.

Tibbits, C. 1999. "Societies with Restricted Liabilities". In *Business Barbados*. St James, Barbados: Miller Publishing.

Todaro, M.P. 1997. *Economic Development*. New York: Longman.

United Nations Commission for Latin America and the Caribbean (UNECLAC). 1995. *Foreign Direct Investment in the Caribbean*. New York: United Nations.

United Nations Conference on Trade and Development (UNCTAD). 2000. *World Investment Report, 2000*. New York: United Nations.

Watson, B. 1974. *Supplementary Notes on Foreign Investment in the Commonwealth Caribbean*. Working Papers, no. 1. Kingston: Institute for Social and Economic Research, University of the West Indies.

Whitehall, P. 1984. "Protection in the Manufacturing Sector of Barbados 1960–1980". *Central Bank of Barbados Economic Review* 11, no. 2 (September).

Whitehall, P., and W. Moore. 2000. "Financing the Small and Micro Business Sector in Barbados". *Central Bank of Barbados Economic Review* 27, no. 3 (December).

Williams, M. 2003. "Globalisation: Some Challenges for the Caribbean in the First Decade of the Twenty First Century". In *Facing Globalisation: Impact and Challenges for Barbados and the Caribbean*, edited by H. Codrington et al. Bridgetown, Barbados: Central Bank of Barbados.

———. 2001. *Managing Public Finances in a Small, Developing Economy: The Case of Barbados*. Westport, CT: Praeger.

Wood, A. 1998. "International Perspectives on Corporate Finance: The Case of Barbados". *Savings and Development*, no. 4.

Worrell, D. 1974. "Determinants of Changes in Commercial Bank Deposits". *Quarterly Report* [Central Bank of Barbados] 1, no. 2 (September).

———. 1982. "An Economic Survey of Barbados, 1946–1980". In *The Economy of Barbados 1946–1980*, edited by D. Worrell. Bridgetown, Barbados: Central Bank of Barbados.

———. 1987. *Small Island Economies: Structure and Performance in the English-Speaking Caribbean Since 1970*. New York: Praeger.

Worrell, D., D. Boamah and T. Campbell. 1996. "The Price Competitiveness of Barbados Exports". *Central Bank of Barbados Economic Review* 23, no. 1 (June).

Worrell, D., K. Greenidge, D. Downes and K. Dalrymple. 1997. *Forecasting Tourism Demand in Barbados*. Working Papers, no. 2. Bridgetown, Barbados: Central Bank of Barbados.

Worrell, D., and R. Prescod. 1983. "The Development of the Financial Sector of Barbados". *Central Bank of Barbados Economic Review* 10.

Zephirin, M.G., and D. Seerattan. 1997. *Financial Innovations in the Caribbean*. St Augustine, Trinidad: University of the West Indies, Caribbean Centre for Monetary Studies.

Zinder, H., and Associates. 1969. *The Future of Tourism in the Eastern Caribbean*. Washington, DC: H. Zinder and Associates.

Index

Note: numbers ending with t refer to tables